18.22

D0031674

DYNAMIC MODERN WOMEN

SCIENTISTS
AND
DOCTORS

Laurie Lindop

Twenty-First Century Books
A Division of Henry Holt and Company
New York

For Jessica Abdow

~≈~

Twenty-First Century Books
A Division of Henry Holt and Company, Inc.
115 West 18th Street
New York, NY 10011

Henry Holt® and colophon are trademarks of
Henry Holt and Company, Inc.
Publishers since 1866

Published in Canada by Fitzhenry & Whiteside Ltd.
195 Allstate Parkway, Markham, Ontario, L3R 4T8

Library of Congress Cataloging-in-Publication Data
Lindop, Laurie.
Scientists and doctors / by Laurie Lindop.
p. cm.— (Dynamic modern women)
Summary: Biographies of ten women in the fields of medicine and science.
Includes bibliographical references and index.
1. Women scientists—Biography—Juvenile literature. 2. Women
medical scientists—Biography—Juvenile literature. 3. Women in
science—Juvenile literature. [1. Scientists. 2. Women—Biography.]
I. Title. II. Series: Lindop, Laurie. Dynamic modern women.
Q141.L6813   1997
509'.2'2   96-41923
[B]—DC20   CIP
                                                                       AC

ISBN 0-8050-4166-4
First Edition—1997

Designed by Kelly Soong

Printed in Mexico.
All first editions are printed on acid-free paper ∞.

1 3 5 7 9 10 8 6 4 2

Photo credits
p. 6: courtesy of Mildred Dresselhaus; p. 16: © Ann Tompkins/Earthwatch; p. 28:
NASA; p. 38: © Cindy Charles; p. 50: © Robert Campbell/National Geographic
Society Image Collection; pp. 62, 108: © AP/Wide World Photos; p. 74: Courtesy
of the National Breast Cancer Coalition; p. 84: © Karsh/Courtesy of The Alan
Mason Chesney Medical Archives of The Johns Hopkins Medical Institutions;
p. 96: AIP Emilio Segré Visual Archives.

CONTENTS

INTRODUCTION

All of the scientists and doctors in this book are women with unlimited vision who have used science to heal the sick, fight disease, and battle social injustice. Many of them have exhibited great courage in following their dreams.

The women of this book dared to look at old problems in new ways, to rethink assumptions, to trust their hunches.

Their stories are ones of triumph against the odds. Often, their discoveries stunned a scientific community that had told them they were attempting the impossible.

One thing they all have in common is that when others told them that they were dreaming too large, they became even more determined to succeed.

ONE

MILDRED DRESSELHAUS

Mildred Dresselhaus works in a variety of topics in solid-state physics. In 1985 she was elected the second woman president of the 40,000 member national organization of professional physicists, The American Physical Society (APS), and in 1997 she will become the president of the American Association for the Advancement of Science.

She has said that although women have "made tremendous strides in the last generation . . . we're still quite a ways from equal opportunity."[1] She is determined to do whatever she can to help level the playing field.

Mildred Dresselhaus knows what it feels like to have the odds stacked against her. She was born on November 11, 1930, in a slum section of Brooklyn, New York. Her parents were poor immigrants who had little education. Often they would go to bed hungry so that Mildred and her brother could eat.

As soon as she was old enough, Mildred began working

after school at any job she could get. For a while she tutored a mentally retarded child and later worked in a factory. When she wasn't working, she was studying. Mildred realized that the surest way out of poverty was a good education.

By the time she entered junior high, she knew that she had a talent for mathematics. She enjoyed using logic and reasoning to find the right answers. Being able to write neat and orderly equations felt like a refuge from the chaos of her school, which she described as a battleground where the strong and tough preyed on the weak. Mildred would always hurry through the hallways, keeping one eye out for possible tormentors.

Education, she also knew, was the key to achieving success. New York City had a remarkable college preparatory institution called Hunter College High School that provided some of the city's best and brightest students with a free education. No one from Mildred's neighborhood had ever been accepted there, and she began studying diligently for the entrance exam.

She passed the test and earned a perfect score on the math section. Exuberant, Mildred entered Hunter High School ready to succeed. She quickly discovered, however, that her junior high school had not adequately prepared her. The other students seemed to be far more advanced in some subjects than she was. In her first semester, she sometimes nearly cried from frustration when her papers received poor grades. But instead of giving up, she decided she would work even harder. By the time she graduated, she was one of the top students in her class and entered Hunter College.

At first Mildred thought she would become an elementary-school teacher. In her freshmen year, however, she took a physics course with a "decisive, no-nonsense, inspirational teacher" named Rosalyn Yalow.[2] Mildred recalled that Dr. Yalow took her aside and said, "Why the hell are *you* in elementary school education?"[3] She realized Mildred had a true knack for scientific inquiry and convinced her to switch her major, though at the time Mildred admitted, "I didn't think I'd achieve much."[4]

Dr. Yalow had different ideas. Even after she had officially resigned from the faculty of Hunter College, she taught for an additional semester simply because she wanted to work a little longer with Mildred Dresselhaus. This was the start of a mentoring relationship that has lasted throughout both women's illustrious careers.

In 1951 Mildred graduated from Hunter summa cum laude and won a Fulbright Fellowship to study at Cambridge University in England. Mildred had applied for the fellowship on a whim after reading an ad, never imagining that she would win.

When she returned to the United States, she received her master's degree at Radcliffe College in 1952. By this time, Mildred knew she wanted to work as a physicist and that to do so she would need to earn a Ph.D. The University of Chicago offered her a job as a teaching assistant so that she could earn money while working on her degree.

Shortly after arriving in Chicago, she was surprised when her adviser tried to discourage her from going into physics. He felt strongly that "a graduate education was a waste of time for women, since most . . . would probably get married."[5] One thing the adviser obviously didn't know about Mildred was that whenever she encountered a challenge, she became obsessed with finding a way to succeed. She informed her adviser that she had absolutely no intention of quitting the program and threw herself into her studies.

Her work at this time was in the relatively new field of solid-state physics. As the name suggests, this type of physics deals with substances in a solid state, as opposed to those in a gaseous or liquid state.

Some of the exciting new work being done in this field focused on semiconductors. A number of different metals can "conduct" electrical currents; this simply means that an electrical current can easily pass through them. Some metals are more effective conductors than others.

The invention of the transistor, which was based on semiconductors, brought about a technological revolution. Before semiconductors, scientists had to use large unwieldy vacuum tubes in electronic circuits. But the small and more efficient semiconducting transistors replaced the vacuum tubes. This, in turn, meant that the machines could shrink in size and increase in working capacity. Semiconductors made possible the invention of the integrated circuit and smaller computers. A computer that would have taken up an entire room was suddenly able to be shrunk down to the size of a briefcase!

Mildred's work at the University of Chicago was in the less studied field of superconductors. In most metal conductors, there are mobile electrons that, when stimulated by electricity, flow through the substance and create a current. Most metals also offer some resistance to this current and the resistance is expressed as heat. To understand this, imagine plugging too many appliances into the same outlet. It will overheat because there is too much current passing through and too much heat being produced because of resistance. Resistance therefore limits the amount of electric power that can be pumped through a particular system without it overheating.

The metals that Mildred was interested in were called superconductors because although they had a relatively high resistance at room temperature (which meant that when electricity passed through them, they became hotter than other metals with lower resistance to electricity, such as copper), at very low temperatures they lost their resistance entirely. The temperature to which they had to be frozen in order to lose their resistance was close to absolute zero (-459.67 degrees Fahrenheit). Near absolute zero the atoms will stop moving in a superconductor. This, in turn, allows the current to pass through without any resistance.

Superconductors are useful when you need to create large currents to do a job. For example, generators for power plants need to be able to transport large currents. Without superconductors, the wires the current needs to pass through would have to be very large. But superconductors let large currents pass through very small wires. In this way, they allow devices that need big currents to be small and compact.

Today their potential uses are still being studied. Obviously the more scientists know about superconductors, the more uses will be found for them. Mildred was interested in learning as much as she could about these fascinating substances.

For her university dissertation, she examined the effect of magnetic fields on superconductors. Such work may seem obscure, but it added to the overall understanding of the properties of superconductors and may prove useful at some point in the future.

She has said, "My own research has been almost exclusively concerned with small science. . . . Progress occurs in many areas in small steps that often seem disconnected. The long-term impact of a given contribution is often difficult to evaluate at the time of discovery."[6]

This is the type of abstract scientific inquiry that Mildred would pursue throughout her career. It is rooted in the quest for accumulating knowledge and answering questions. Like a detective searching for clues, she would find some clues that would prove immediately useful, others that would be filed away for possible future use. She would also pursue a few dead ends or false leads.

As soon as she earned her Ph.D., Mildred received a number of job offers. Since she had decided to marry a fellow physicist named Gene Dresselhaus, she joined him at Cornell

University, where Mildred won a fellowship from the National Science Foundation. A year later, their first child was born.

In 1960 Mildred and her husband accepted positions at the Lincoln Laboratory at the Massachusetts Institute of Technology (M.I.T.) in Cambridge, Massachusetts. The M.I.T. lab specialized in semiconductors. Much of Mildred's work there was in the properties of semimetals, which have properties somewhere between those of semiconductors and metals. She also continued her work on the properties of materials at high magnetic fields at M.I.T.'s Francis Bitter National Magnet Laboratory, where machines could produce magnetic fields that were 100,000 times more powerful than that of the magnetic field on earth.

Much of her research resulted in the development of advanced materials for products. For example, some of her work is currently being directed toward the development of batteries that will last longer. Other aspects of her research are being used to find ways to more efficiently cool things such as household refrigerators and other devices. Dr. Dresselhaus has said that often companies will come to her to ask what she is working on with the hope that they can use her discoveries to design new products or improve older ones. In 1968 M.I.T. recognized her achievements by making her a full professor.

In many ways it is remarkable that Mildred was able to accomplish as much as she did because during this time she was trying to raise four children. She said, "I never took any time off to have the kids. They just sort of worked into my schedule."[7] Still, there were times when she would have to wait at home until the baby-sitter arrived in the mornings and would be an hour late getting to work. She found that "the attitude of her male colleagues was not at all supportive of her difficulty; rather they were critical."[8]

When Mildred started teaching at M.I.T. in 1967, there were only a few women in her classes. At the time, "it was unusual for women students to ask questions in class or to participate in class discussions," she said. "As the number of women students increased, they participated more and more, and in very recent years their class participation has become essentially indistinguishable from that of the men."[9]

Mildred felt it was crucial to bring more women into the science program and, with the help of other female colleagues, formed the Women's Forum at M.I.T. This group addressed the concerns of women students and faculty. It helped push through affirmative action programs, so that now, Mildred said, "If we have two applicants of equal ability, we give the benefit of the doubt to a woman."[10] In a short time, more and more women were being admitted to M.I.T.

Mildred felt that another way she could help women to succeed was by serving as a mentor and role model to her female students. In a university system where professors often put their own research above the needs of students, Mildred made a commitment to get to know her students and to foster their careers. She would encourage her female students to trust their hunches and take more scientific risks; she had noticed that female students sometimes had more difficulty doing this than did their male peers. Mildred would remind her female students that many important scientific discoveries were made only because scientists were willing to rely on their instincts and question some long-held assumptions.

In 1972 Mildred was promoted to Associate Department Head of Electrical Engineering at M.I.T. This job entailed a good deal of administrative responsibility, and she was afraid she would not do a good job. Later, she admitted, "I never told that to anyone."[11] She quickly proved that being an administrator came as easily to her as scientific inquiry.

Nine years later, she said she was "caught completely by surprise when the chairman of the APS [American Physical Society] nominating committee called to ask if I would run for vice-president. . . . I could hardly believe that I was a serious candidate."[12] But once again, Mildred surprised herself. After discussing the proposal with her husband and children, she agreed to run.

Mildred ran against a very distinguished physicist with a long history of leadership in the field. Her platform called for the creation of more opportunities for young scientists. She also supported intensified work to increase the general public's understanding of physics so that average citizens could better understand the impact of advances in science on their lives. This platform reflects her belief that science should be inclusive and accessible to everyone—no matter what level of expertise or committment a person brings to the subject.

Although Mildred wondered if her platform was too liberal and too activist for her to win, she defeated her opponent. After one year as vice-president and another as president-elect, she became president of the society in 1984.

As president, Mildred continued the society's work on studying such important national issues as the Strategic Defense Initiative and nuclear safety. She also was involved with the completion of a massive survey of the exciting discoveries in physics during the past decade, as well as an analysis of the most promising research opportunities for the upcoming decade.

This experience, she said, "helped me see more connections between the work of our research group at M.I.T. and some of the major thrusts of this decade. . . . The small patchwork pieces discovered in a multitude of small groups somehow fit together to form a large, beautiful, patchwork quilt."[13]

In 1985 she helped author an important survey of women graduate students at M.I.T., which was later published in *Physics Today*. She found what she had long suspected—that despite numerous improvements in opportunities for women, inequities still existed. "Women physics students tended to work harder, feel more pressure and believed that they get less help than men do . . . ," she stated in the report. "Twenty percent of women graduate students in physics felt that their sex made it more difficult for them to succeed."[14] She hoped that the report would make professors all over the country more aware of the unique problems facing women graduate students and inspire them to implement changes.

In 1985 Dresselhaus was given the highest honor possible at M.I.T. when she became the first woman to be named an institute professor. Since then she has continued to teach and work at M.I.T. In 1990 she was awarded the National Medal of Science and in 1996 was elected the president of the American Association for the Advancement of Science. This is the world's largest science organization, and she hopes to use her position to help push for greater improvements in opportunities for female scientists, as well as for all young scientists.

She said that the advice she would give to any student interested in going into science would be to "follow your interests, get the best available education and training, set your sights high, be persistent, be flexible, keep your options open, accept help when offered, and be prepared to help others."[15]

T W O

Biruté Galdikas

It is five-thirty in the morning and Biruté Galdikas (pronounced bi-ROO-tay GALL-di-kus) climbs out of her hammock and slips down to the floor of the rain forest. As she walks by, thousands of inch-long leeches attracted to her body's warmth wiggle toward her and try to attach themselves to her legs. The humidity is stifling even this early in the morning, and she uses a towel to mop the sweat from her face. Biruté slogs waist-deep through the black waters of the swamp, swatting at hordes of mosquitoes until she reaches her destination, a seemingly unremarkable tree. She unrolls her grass mat and sits down to wait. As the sun rises, there's a stirring in the uppermost branches, and a few moments later a hairy red orangutan emerges, yawning. Biruté opens her notebook and gets ready to record her observations.

Twenty-five years ago, Biruté Galdikas embarked on her study of the orangutans in the Borneo rain forests. She is the first scientist ever to make a long-term study of their life habits, and her research has revolutionized our understanding of these endangered creatures who are considered the most elusive of all the great apes.

Biruté Galdikas was born in Wiesbaden, West Germany, on May 10, 1946. Her parents were Lithuanians who fled after the Soviet occupation of their country at the end of World War II. When Biruté was a toddler, her family moved to Toronto, Ontario, where her father worked as a miner, machinist, and house painter. Biruté's mother worked as a nurse.

As a child, Biruté loved the outdoors. She would spend hours exploring the local park. "I remember it as a vast, wild place," she said, "where one could follow little streams under trailing willows and find huge land turtles and nesting mallard ducks."[1]

During high school, Biruté became interested in orangutans. They struck her as resembling our earliest prehistoric ancestors. But she could find only very limited information about these intriguing creatures. Perhaps, one day, she thought, she would be able to find a way to study these great red apes.

In 1965 Birute entered the University of California at Los Angeles (UCLA). She majored in psychology and also took courses in zoology, ancient history, and anthropology.

After receiving her undergraduate degree in psychology summa cum laude, she joined UCLA's graduate school program in anthropology and began researching ways to study orangutans. In 1969 Louis Leakey came to lecture at UCLA. The husband of Mary Leakey, he was stout, with tousled white hair. The couple were considered one of the great archaeologist teams of all time.

Leakey believed that the fossilized remains he and his wife had found of our earliest prehuman ancestors told only half the story. These fossils showed what our ancestors looked like, but not how they lived. In order to understand the social life of our prehistoric relatives, Louis proposed a series of long-term studies of humankind's closest living relatives, the great apes.

Scientists believe that millions of years ago humans shared a common ancestor with the great apes. The modern-day great apes include the gorillas and chimpanzees of Africa and the orangutans of Asia. Ten to fourteen million years ago, orangutans branched off from this common ancestor, and today, 97 percent of their genetic material is identical to that of humans. Gorillas branched off somewhat later, and chimpanzees branched off only five million years ago. In fact, chimpanzees and humans share almost 99 percent of their genetic material, which means that a human could receive a blood transfusion from a chimpanzee.

Leakey reasoned that if we could understand how the great apes live today, we might begin to understand the lives of our apelike ancestors. This was a controversial theory that was further complicated by the assumptions of many scientists that it would be virtually impossible for a researcher to get close enough to collect data on these elusive creatures in the wild. But Louis was convinced that not only was it possible, but that women would be unusually well suited for the task. He believed that women were better observers than men and that they would be less aggressive and thus less intrusive around their subjects.

By the time Leakey came to speak at UCLA, he had sent Jane Goodall to Gombe, Africa, and the scientific world was stunned by her startling, groundbreaking reports about the wild chimpanzees. At the lecture Biruté attended, Leakey said that another one of his protégés, Dian Fossey, had just telegraphed saying that "the mountain gorillas are becoming so habituated to her presence that one is even untying her shoelaces."[2]

Trying to control her excitement, Biruté waited until the

end of the lecture when everyone else had left the audi-toruium bcfore going up to Leakey and telling him about her dream of studying orangutans.

"Dr. Leakey looked at me very coldly and didn't say much," she recalled. "I could have been telling him he had dandruff for all his interest."[3] But Biruté persevered and eventually convinced Dr. Leakey that she was absolutely serious, that this was her lifelong dream, and he agreed to help her launch her study.

Orangutans originated in Africa but then moved to Asia. At one time they ranged throughout Southeast Asia and into China, but today there are fewer than 30,000, and they live only in the rain forests of two Indonesian islands, Borneo and Sumatra. They are semi-solitary and the only great apes who are "arboreal," which means they spend most of their time in the trees. There are enormous physical difference between orangutan males and females. The female orangs grow to be about three and one-half feet tall and weigh on average sev-enty pounds. The males, on the other hand, can be almost five feet tall and weigh as much as one hundred and fifty pounds. The adult males have thick cheek pads around their faces and a pouch at their throats that they can inflate when they want to make a territorial hoot, known as a "long call."

Very few scientists before Biruté Galdikas had ever at-tempted to study the wild orangutans. The climate and dan-gers of the Borneo rain forests had defeated a number of researchers. And the apes' solitary shyness also made them hard to spot. During one two-month study not a single wild orangutan had been sighted.

Biruté, however, was determined to break this discourag-ing pattern. Getting to Borneo proved to be her first obstacle. It took Louis two and one-half years to raise the $9,000 needed to launch her research. During this time, Biruté tried not to lose hope and studied the orangutans at the Los Ange-les Zoo, went on an archaeological dig to Yugoslavia, and married her boyfriend, Rod Brindamour, a Canadian who was eager to accompany her into the wilds.

Finally, in November 1971, Biruté and Rod arrived in Indonesia with only a couple of backpacks and some photographic equipment. Their destination was Tanjung Puting, a large nature reserve on a peninsula on the coast of Borneo. Most of the interior of the reserve had never been explored.

To get to the reserve, she and Rod and a few forestry workers rode in a small motorboat up the steamy Sekonyer River. The temperature was ninety degrees, and a monsoon rain drummed on the thick leaves of the trees clogging the banks. Clouds of mosquitoes swarmed over the water's surface. Everything smelled of mold and rot and swamp.

"The most distinctive sensation of the rain forest," Birute said, "is the oppressive humidity, which weighs down the frail human frame like a ball and chain."[f] Even in the rain, Biruté felt almost as though the humidity were suffocating her.

It was dark by the time they docked in what seemed like the middle of nowhere. An abandoned hut was to become their home. In the beam of her flashlight, she saw swarms of spiders, some as big as her hand.

"It did not look particularly appetizing," Biruté recalled.[5]

At dawn the next morning, Biruté set out with her binoculars and a notebook to find some orangutans. Rod grabbed a machete to clear paths. It didn't take long for them to discover that the forest was "booby-trapped" with dangers. Reaching up to grab a branch, they would find it was really a snake. Poisonous caterpillars dropped from the trees. Logs oozed acidic sap that could burn the skin. Sharp toothed crocodiles hid in the swamps and rivers. And everywhere were leeches. "Fat black leeches, bloated with our blood, dropped out of our socks and off our necks and fell out of our underwear," Biruté recalled.[6]

These felt like minor irritations, however, compared to her increasing frustration at not finding any orangutans. Biruté got a fleeting glimpse of one on her second day, but after that, nothing. Day after day, she went out but found no orangutans.

It may seem that it would be easy to spot a large, red hairy creature, but up in the trees the leaf cover was so dense that no sunlight could penetrate. In the shadows, the orangutans' red hair was muted into a dull blackish color. Even if Biruté were to stare directly at one, it might look like nothing more than a lumpy shadow.

Finally, she spotted a young male orangutan up in a tree eating bark. He hissed at her but didn't run. She watched him for five straight hours. "It was as if she were drinking in the orangutan, indulging herself as she studied every pursing of its lips, every chew, every faraway gaze, every scratch."[7]

After that Biruté gradually began to discover ways to more easily track orangutans. Rinds of fruit or cracked-open nuts at the base of a tree were often clues to an orangutan's presence. Also, she learned to look for unusual shapes in the trees and to listen. The telltale crash of branches, the thud of fruit falling, or the male's territorial "long calls" could all indicate an ape's presence.

As she began to find apes more regularly, Biruté decided to imitate Jane Goodall's system of giving members of the same family (whenever it was possible to determine this) names that began with the same letter. Using this system, she gave the name Bert to the female orangutan Beth's baby. Sometimes she also used distinguishing characteristics to name the animals. For example, she called an orangutan who had an especially large throat patch under his chin Throatpouch, or TP.

This system was in contrast with the traditional scientific protocol of identifying animals by numbers. But like Jane Goodall, Biruté felt that each ape deserved a real name. They were not statistics to her; they were individuals with unique personalities.

In order to intimately know the animals, Birute had to "habituate" them, which meant she had to get the subjects so accustomed to her presence that they would go about their activities as if she were not there. No other researcher had ever managed this feat with orangutans, but Biruté was determined to succeed. And she did.

The first adolescent orangutan Biruté habituated was named Georgina. "Georgina was an exquisite creature," Biruté wrote. "Her long hair parted in the middle almost as if it had been styled. . . . Her narrow delicate face was dominated by large, liquid brown eyes with thick lashes."[8] She was also the first orangutan to show any interest in her human observer. The other orangutans Biruté encountered were irritated by her presence and would show their frustration by kiss-squeaking, dropping branches, defecating, or even trying to push over trees on top of her. But Georgina was different.

Once, after Biruté had been observing her for a number of days, Georgina climbed down a tree until she was a few feet from Biruté and Rod. She stared at them with great curiosity. This was Biruté's first close look at a wild orangutan, although at that moment it was hard to tell who was more intent on studying whom. Biruté later came to realize that Georgina's behavior was an expression of the friendly curiosity that is typical of many orangutan adolescents.

Like human teenagers, these female and male adolescent apes (from age three to about eight when they reach adulthood) enjoyed hanging out together and would sometimes travel in a group. As adults, however, the orangutans spent most of their time alone.

We humans are naturally social creatures, and to us such a life might seem lonely. But Biruté found that since orangutans ate mainly fruit, bark, and insects, it made sense for them to forage alone. If they moved in a group, they would soon strip a tree of its food and then have to move on in search of another tree. A single orangutan, however, could spend hours in one tree eating the fruit without having to move.

During her first few years in the forest, Biruté managed to catalog an unprecedented study of 400 different types of food she witnessed orangutans eating. She also discovered that the apes seemed to know exactly which trees were bearing ripe fruit and that this knowledge was not "innate" (something they were born with). Rather, the apes had to learn this information from their mothers. On average a wild orangutan female gives birth only once every eight years and bears three or fewer offspring in her lifetime. A young orangutan will remain in almost constant physical contact with its mother from birth until adolescence. The mother teaches the baby all the skills of survival, including which fruits to eat and how to eat them.

Orangutan mothers also teach their young to build nests. These nests are quite complicated structures constructed of long, thin leaves. Orangutans usually build a new one each night. Biruté would sometimes laugh watching baby orangutans practice building nests that would turn out hopelessly lopsided and messy.

Biruté discovered that many baby orangutans were being illegally captured and sold on the black market to unauthorized persons, zoos, and circuses around the world. In order to capture a baby orangutan, the mother usually had to be killed because she never lets her baby out of her sight.

When Biruté arrived, the Indonesian government had outlawed this practice, yet the law was rarely enforced. Biruté and Rod decided to do something about it and enlisted the help of forestry officials. In fact, the first Indonesian phrase that Rod learned was, "This officer is here with me so he can confiscate your orangutan."9

Indonesians do not like confrontations and would usually surrender their pets without much complaint. Biruté and Rod would take the baby apes back to the camp with the hope of rehabilitating them to the wild.

The first ape she saved was named Sugito. He was too young to be on his own and immediately adopted Biruté as his substitute mother. He would cling to her night and day as he was accustomed to doing to his orangutan mother. When Biruté would try to peel him off, he'd let out screams of distress. Sugito also insisted on sleeping in bed with Rod and Biruté, but would not be potty trained. "A good night's sleep was impossible," she said. "I would be awoken repeatedly by a warm . . . liquid drenching me. . . . Yet I knew if I got up to change clothes Sugito would immediately wake up and start howling."[10]

Despite these problems, she could not help but fall in love with the little ball of fluff. Soon after Sugito arrived, other ex-captive orangs joined the camp. "Sometimes I felt as though I were surrounded by wild, unruly children in orange suits who had not yet learned their manners," Biruté laughed.[11] The orphans got into everything. They would rip mattresses, swing from the ceiling, drink shampoo, and suck the fountain pens dry.

In 1976 Biruté gave birth to her son, Binti. "It took my own child . . . to remind me of the deep evolutionary differences between humans and orangutans, even though we are so strikingly similar," Biruté admitted. [12] Humans have three times the brain capacity of orangs, and she began to notice the developmental differences between her son and the orphan apes.

The orangs made great playmates for baby Binti. He'd take baths, wrestle, and play with them. Soon his parents realized that their son was starting to imitate the apes' behavior. He was kiss-squeaking, mimicking the orangs' facial expressions, and trying to climb trees.

It was clear that Binti needed human playmates. In 1977

and 1978, the family left Borneo for extended visits to Los Angeles. Biruté was working on her dissertation for her Ph.D., which, when she finished, was 333 pages long and dedicated to Louis Leakey (who had died). It was enthusiastically received and some reviewers called it "monumental."[13]

Although she enjoyed the comforts of Los Angeles, Biruté was anxious to return to Borneo. Rod, on the other hand, was not. Years of suffering from festering tropical ulcers had left permanent purple holes in his legs. The retinas of his eyes were becoming detached from constant use of antimalarial drugs. He felt like he had put his life on hold. "Rod didn't have a career, a car, a credit card or a degree," Biruté said. "All he had to show for seven and a half years in the jungle was a bunch of pictures of orangutans."[14]

When the family returned to Borneo, his dissastisfaction deepened. A year later, he announced that he was going to Canada and wanted Binti to go with him. Rod also told Biruté that he had fallen in love with Binti's Indonesian baby-sitter. They planned to be married after he got a divorce. Biruté knew that she wanted to stay in Borneo with the orangs and made the heart-wrenching decision to let her son leave with his father. Today Rod is a computer systems analyst and Binti is a typical North American teenager.

After they left, Biruté decided to hire a number of local Dayak workers to help her. The Dayaks were members of an ancient rain forest tribe. They had a natural talent for tracking orangs and knew them better than any other Indonesians did. Two years after Rod left, Biruté married a Dayak named Pak Bohap. They had two children, Frederick and Jane. During the week, the children would live with their father in the Dayak village and play with other children. On the weekends, they would visit their mother at the camp.

Today the camp has grown to seven buildings. Most of its funding comes from Earthwatch, a Boston based conservation group that sends volunteers to work with Biruté Galdikas.

Most come home delighted with their adventures and their encounters with the orangutan orphans. These orphans are not the original ones Biruté rescued, but a new group. Most of the older ones, like Sugito, have been successfully rehabilitated into the wild and only come around to visit periodically.

In recent years, Biruté has had to fight logging companies that threaten to destroy the trees which are home to many orangs. Through her battles to save the environment, Biruté has made a number of powerful enemies. In 1991 forestry officials almost refused to renew her permit to work in the reserve. At the last moment, however, she managed to convince the government to grant her the necessary documents.

Since then, there have been concerns about her safety, but she is determined to continue to study her beloved orangs, to fight to save orphans, and to work to preserve their environment. Despite the tremendous amount of research she has compiled, there are still many questions about the apes that Biruté wants to answer.

"There's one female," she said, "that I've known since she was born. And now she's pregnant. I might be around when she dies."[15] That could be quite a long time since orangutans can live to age sixty or older!

THREE

MAE
JEMISON

When Mae Jemison was a little girl she wanted to be an astronaut. It seemed an impossible dream because she was black, and all the astronauts then were white men. But her motto was "Don't be limited by others' limited imaginations."[1]

On September 12, 1992, after years of hard work and preparation, Mae Jemison walked out to the launchpad at Kennedy Space Center in her orange NASA space suit and waved to the cheering crowd. She was about to become the first African-American woman in space. Although she was proud of her achievement, she also felt that it must be put into perspective. "I'm very aware of the fact that I'm not the first African-American woman who had the skills, the talent, the desire to be an astronaut," she said. "I happen to be the first one that NASA selected."[2]

Mae Carol Jemison was born on October 17, 1956, in Decatur, Alabama, the youngest of three children. When she was four, the family moved to Chicago. Her father was a roofer and carpenter who, before retiring, took a job as the supervisor of janitorial services at a charity organization. Her mother was a schoolteacher. Mae said, "My parents have always been supportive of me. When I was a child, they put up with all kinds of stuff, like science projects, dance classes, and art lessons. They encouraged me to do it, and they would find the money, time, and energy to help me be involved."[3]

One of her favorite subjects was science. She said, "I went through a phase, when I was probably from ten to fourteen years old, where I read lots and lots of astronomy books, not science fiction, but actually astronomy books."[4] On summer nights she liked to lie outside and stare up at the stars.

In 1969 she followed with great excitement the news reports of the Apollo 11 mission to the moon. The astronauts on board—Neil Armstrong, Michael Collins, and Edwin Aldrin—were her heroes. They were white men with crew cuts, and although she respected their heroics, she was nevertheless furious that NASA had excluded women and African Americans from their program. This began to change in the 1970s with pressure from the growing civil rights and women's rights movements, but it would take until 1983 before the first woman, Sally Ride, ventured into space.

Mae knew the odds were stacked against her, but she was determined that one day she would find a way to break through the discriminatory barriers and travel into outer space. On her favorite television program, Star Trek, the communications officer was Lieutenant Uhura, a black woman. If an African-American woman could be an astronaut in television's fictional universe, Mae thought, why not in real life?

Mae was an outstanding student and attended Morgan Park High School on Chicago's South Side. One of Mae's classmates recalled, "We knew if we didn't raise our hands, the teacher would go to Mae for the answer to the problem."[5] Mae's parents had taught her to be proud of her African-

American heritage, and she never hesitated to share her knowledge or viewpoints with her teachers or classmates.

In 1973 Mae graduated from high school at the age of sixteen and entered Stanford University on a National Achievement Scholarship. She majored in chemical engineering and African-American studies. It was very important to her to be a well-rounded person. She said, "I truly feel someone interested in science is interested in understanding what's going on in the world. That means you have to find out about social science, art, and politics."[6] Mae joined dance and theater productions, played intramural football, and was elected president of the black student union.

In 1977 during her final year at Stanford, NASA announced it was looking for candidates, including women, for the space-shuttle program. NASA had hired the actress who played Mae's childhood hero, Lieutenant Uhura, to recruit women scientists from the universities and private sector.

Of course, Mae was pleased that NASA was finally giving women access to the space program, but she did not feel that the time was right for her to apply. Becoming an astronaut wasn't something she could plan her future around because the chance of succeeding was so small. She felt that it would be wiser first to establish a more stable career in medicine and then, at a later date, try to join NASA's program.

After graduating from Stanford in 1977, Mae entered Cornell University Medical College in New York City. She served as the president of the Cornell chapter of the National Student Medical Association. Through this organization she worked in medical facilities in Cuba, Kenya, and Thailand. At times this work was difficult and dangerous, but she said, "When I was in the refugee camp in Thailand, I learned more about medicine there than I could have in a lifetime somewhere else. I refuse to think those people owe me any thanks. I got a lot out of it."[7]

After receiving her medical degree in 1981, Mae decided

to join the Peace Corps as a medical officer in the West African countries of Sierra Leone and Liberia. At the age of twenty-six, she was in charge of ministering to the medical needs of the Peace Corps volunteers and U.S. embassy employees. She said, "I was one of the youngest doctors over there and I had to learn to deal with how people reacted to my age while asserting myself as a physician."[8] In addition to treating patients and administering the medical program, she wrote manuals for self-care and developed research projects.

The associate director of the program recalled that Mae was "an interesting young lady . . . a dynamic person . . . and how knowledgeable she was in areas as different as medicine, cooking, and dance."[9] Mae loved learning about African culture and enjoyed dressing in the ethnic style. The director said, "She got deeply involved in the lives of local children, even paying for one boy's schooling."[10]

After a two-year tour of duty, Mae returned to the States and in 1985 joined a health plan as a physician. She had not, however, forgotten her dream of being an astronaut and decided to apply to the space program. Two years earlier, NASA had taken the big step of sending the first woman, Sally Ride, and the first African-American, Guion Bluford Jr., into space on board the space shuttle.

The space shuttle was designed by NASA in the 1970s as the first reusable spacecraft. The shuttle looks like a rocket on takeoff, but when it returns to Earth it lands on a runway like an airplane. The space shuttle has been used to repair and launch satellites and as a laboratory for experiments in space. Mae hoped to become a mission specialist astronaut in charge of experiments on board, as opposed to a pilot astronaut who actually flies the shuttle.

All astronauts must meet the basic qualifications of a degree in math, engineering, or biological or physical science, plus three years of related work. A medical degree would count toward those three years of experience. Astronauts must also be physically fit and have eyesight that is correctable to 20/20.

Mae knew she met these basic qualifications but began taking additional night classes in engineering to bolster her already impressive résumé. On January 28,1986, three months after submitting her application, Mae was watching the launch of the space shuttle *Challenger* on television. She saw the rocket boosters fire and the ship rise into the sky. A moment later there was a massive explosion. Mae felt her stomach knot and thought, "Well, they must have bailed out. There must be survivors." [11] But there were not. The entire crew had been killed, including black astronaut Ronald McNair.

After the horrible accident, NASA postponed the selection process until October 1986. Although Mae was terribly saddened by what had happened, it did not prevent her from wanting to go into space. She passed the first phase of the selection process and went to NASA's Johnson Space Center in Houston, Texas, for a thorough medical examination and background check.

Then, on June 4, 1987, Mae was told on the phone by a NASA official that she was one of fifteen applicants chosen out of a pool of 2,000. "I was very happy . . ." Mae recalled. "I didn't jump up and down and do a dance, but yes, I was very excited."[12] She was the first African-American woman admitted to the astronaut program. Mae moved to Houston to begin a year of intensive training. This training, she said, was "principally academic—studying procedures, the space shuttle, the hardware we work with, etc."[13]

Because an astronaut must be able to handle crisis situations, Mae and the other candidates took part in wilderness and water survival training. They also went on airplane flights that simulated the weightlessness of outer space. The special training jet would climb almost straight up into the air and then fall into a nosedive. During the dive, the passengers became weightless for about thirty seconds and floated around in a padded room.

Jemison completed the training program in August of 1988 and officially qualified as a mission-specialist astronaut. However, she worked at NASA for another five years before being scheduled to make her first space flight. The mission, called STS-47 Spacelab J, was part of a joint venture between the United States and Japan to conduct experiments in life sciences and materials processing in outer space. In the months leading up to the launch, Mae worked with scientists from both countries, designing the experiments that would be conducted during the flight.

Some of the experiments were of particular interest to women. "In space humans lose calcium from the bones," Jemison explained. "You start seeing the effect after ten or twelve days. Women are more prone to osteoporosis [calcium loss], but we don't have a lot of data on women. The longest a woman has been up is ten days. Does this mean that we should be wary about sending women up for long periods? The real issue is how to keep people healthy while they're in space."[14]

On September 12, 1992, the day of her launch, Mae ate breakfast with the six other astronauts on her crew. Then she went with them to put on her bulky orange space suit and climb aboard the van that drove them to the launchpad. As she walked onto the launchpad to the cheers of the crowd, Mae paused while the other astronauts boarded the ship and stood looking around at Kennedy Space Center. Her childhood dream was about to come true.

"I was thinking," she said later, "that if I had been a little girl and I knew that this was going to happen, I'd be jumping up and down, grinning and smiling."[15]

After the crew strapped themselves into their seats, they had to wait two-and-a-half hours while NASA technicians prepared for liftoff. During this time, Mae tried not to think about the *Challenger* shuttle disaster. She wondered what her friends and family who had come to the launch were thinking. It helped to know they were there watching her.

At 10:23 A.M. the rocket boosters fired. Mae's mother cried, "My baby's on top of an inferno!"[16] But as the shuttle roared up into the sky and flew out of sight without a hitch, she grabbed her husband and began crying with relief. Mae Jemison had brought on board with her a poster from the all-black Alvin Ailey dance troupe, a flag that had flown over the Organization of African Unity, a banner from Alpha Kappa Alpha (the oldest black sorority in the country), and a banner from the Mae C. Jemison Academy (an alternative public school in Detroit that had been named after her).

"What I was trying to do with my collection of items," she said, "was represent people who haven't been invited to be part of space exploration."[17] For herself, Mae brought a little voodoo statue she'd gotten in Sierra Leone, a Michael Jordan jersey from the Chicago Bulls basketball team, and lots of her favorite music tapes.

During her eight days in space, Mae was very busy. She began her work shifts with a quote from her childhood television hero, Lieutenant Uhura, "Hailing frequencies open!"[18]

In addition to her experiments with osteoporosis, she was in charge of studying a new way of controlling motion sickness. The results of the study were eagerly awaited by space centers all over the world because half of all astronauts experience motion sickness, and the drugs that are commonly used to relieve it can cause drowsiness. Unlike the rest of the *Endeavor* crew, Mae did not take these drugs to control nausea. Instead, she used her training in biofeedback techniques, which rely upon the use of meditation and relaxation exercises to control the body's functions. The results of her experiment proved inconclusive, but researchers hope to continue to study the usefulness of biofeedback in space travel.

In another experiment, Mae studied the effect of weight-lessness on the fertilization of frogs. She hatched tadpoles and found that they showed no ill effects from their weight-less condition. "Frogs," Mae said, "like other life-forms, take so much of their basic knowledge from the environment, we were curious . . . if they would turn out to be . . . well, normal frogs."[19]

Mae had very little free time in space. Almost every five-minute period was carefully scheduled. But each day there was an hour and a half of open time when she would look out the window and stargaze. "You could also see the southern lights," she said. "They streak up to the shuttle—just like cur-tains, sheer curtains of light that streak up. It's beautiful."[20]

During the flight, Mae was surprised by how calm she felt. She thought she might have been more anxious about the fact that there was only a window separating her from the in-hospitable environment of outer space. But, she said, "I actu-ally felt that I would have loved to have been up there by myself in a big glass bubble. If I had imagined myself travel-ing through space in this glass bubble to another star, it would have been perfectly OK."[21]

On September 20, 1992, the *Endeavor* landed at Kennedy Space Center. The crew had traveled 3.3 million miles and or-bited the earth 127 times.

After the mission, Mae moved back to Chicago. She was a celebrity, and for six days there were parades and parties in her honor. She received many awards, including the Ebony Black Achievement Award and the Essence Science and Tech-nology Award. In 1993 she was inducted into the National Women's Hall of Fame.

Mae hopes that her work will inspire other women and African Americans to get involved with space exploration. "It's our right," she has said. "This is one area where we can get in on the ground floor and possibly help to direct where space exploration will go in the future. . . . If we're not there from the beginning, helping to determine what happens to these re-sources, we'll have no say in how they are to be used."[22]

A few months after her mission, Mae took a leave of ab-sence from NASA to teach at Dartmouth College in New Hampshire. On March 8, 1993, she officially resigned from the astronaut corps. She said that although she still loved space exploration, the schedule at NASA was rigorous and "there were other things I wanted to do."[23]

In the summer of 1994, she helped institute the Interna-tional Science Camp at Choate Rosemary Hall, a private prep school in Connecticut. The goal of the camp was to help young people look at science not as simply equations to be solved and data to be memorized, but as a way of developing a sense of how things fit together in the world. Mae wanted the camp also "to change the way people look at scien-tists. . . . We want . . . kids to say, 'Hey, this is all right.'"[24]

Jemison also formed a company called the Jemison Group, which would seek space-age solutions to technologi-cal problems in developing countries. The Jemison Group's first project was to establish satellite communications to en-sure better health-care services for the people of West Africa.

She feels it is important for children to follow their dreams. "Society has oftentimes told people who look like me that they can't succeed," she said. "It's important not only for a little black girl growing up to know, 'Yeah, you can become an astronaut because here's Mae Jemison,' but it's [also] im-portant for older white males who sometimes make decisions on those careers of those little black girls."[25]

When Mae thinks about all that she has accomplished, she feels that, more than anything, her success is due to the fact that she was never afraid to tackle a challenge. She said, "I always figured if someone else could do it, so could I, and if no one else had tried it, what the hell, I would."[26]

FOUR

MARY-CLAIRE KING

At the end of a meeting of geneticists in Cincinnati, Ohio, in October 1990, geneticist Mary-Claire King stepped up to the microphone to give an unscheduled presentation. She announced that she had found the location of the gene that predisposes women to breast cancer. Suddenly the room was abuzz with excitement. Most scientists had thought that finding the gene was impossible, but for nineteen years Mary-Claire had been diligently plodding ahead. Whenever she would get discouraged, she would think of the 600,000 women in the United States who are affected by this disease. "I really do think that science can do good things for people," she has said. "But I also think you have to set out to do it that way."[1]

At the end of a meeting of geneticists in Cincinnati, Ohio, in

Mary-Claire King was born on February 27, 1946, in Wilmette, Illinois, a suburb of Chicago. She always loved mysteries, solving puzzles, and the study of mathematics. In 1963, she entered Carleton College in Northfield, Minnesota, as a math major. After three years, she earned her bachelors degree, was elected to the honor society Phi Beta Kappa, and graduated cum laude.

She was only twenty years old, but was already convinced that she wanted to use "what I knew how to do in a relevant way."[2] She decided to pursue graduate studies in biostatistics at the University of California at Berkeley and hoped to apply her mathematical skills to help solve problems in medical research. But then, on a whim, she enrolled in a course on genetics. Genetics is the science that studies genes and heredity. In a cell's nucleus, genes are organized into strings of DNA called chromosomes. Everyone inherits twenty-three pairs of chromosomes from his or her parents. Each gene codes for a certain protein that is important to maintaining healthy cells.

Mary-Claire would listen with fascination as her genetics professor began each class by highlighting a great puzzle about heredity. At first the puzzle would seem unsolvable, but as he described the calculations, clues, and leaps of logic that researchers had used to eventually answer the question, it would seem that the solution was inevitable. Mary-Claire realized that genetics was like solving crossword puzzles and mysteries. Also, it had the potential to help people in a much more direct way than abstract math. She immediately changed her area of concentration to genetics.

While she was at Berkeley, the Vietnam War was escalating and Mary-Claire, like many other young people, felt the United States should pull out of the war. The university was at the tumultuous forefront of the student antiwar movement, and she recalled, "We were working against the war and being tear gassed on the way to lab. When we weren't on our way to the lab, we were demonstrating and picketing."[3]

In 1969 increasingly virulent antiwar protests on the Berkeley campus led Ronald Reagan, then the governor of

California, to call in the National Guard. Watching the troops storm the campus, Mary-Claire despaired. She felt it was impossible for her to go back to studying science in the ivory tower of the university when all around her society seemed to be in turmoil. Mary-Claire decided to take time off from graduate school and go to work for the consumer activist and lawyer Ralph Nader. She threw herself into a project studying the effects of pesticides on farmworkers.

At the end of her leave of absence, she returned to Berkeley. She hoped to work on a doctoral project that would prove helpful to people. One of her ideas was to study the effect of human exposure to DNA-damaging chemicals in the environment. But her imagination far outdistanced the technologies available at the time, and all of the projects she proposed proved unworkable.

Frustrated, she considered quitting her studies to take a full-time job with Ralph Nader. But before she did this, she sought advice from her friend and mentor Allan Wilson, a professor of biochemistry and molecular biology at Berkeley. She confided that she could never get her experiments to work, and he responded, "If everyone whose experiments failed stopped doing science, there wouldn't be any science."[4]

He invited her to work with him in his laboratory. He was investigating a theory that humans and chimpanzees diverged from a common ancestor about five million years ago. He encouraged Mary-Claire to use her skills as a mathematician and geneticist to study the differences between chimps and humans. After numerous experiments, she discovered, much to her own surprise, that the two species have more than 99 percent of DNA in common. This work not only earned her a Ph.D., but her paper cowritten with Wilson was eventually published with much acclaim as the cover article in the April 1975 issue of *Science* magazine.

The summer after she completed her doctorate, she married ecologist Robert Colwell and took a job teaching science at the Universidad de Chile in Santiago. She fell in love with the country, which struck her as stunningly beautiful. However, the beauty and peace were shattered on September 11, 1973, when a violent military coup killed the head of the government, Salvador Allende Gossens. The insurgents went on a bloody crusade and murdered suspected leftists, including students and faculty at the university.

"It was hell," Mary-Claire recalled, her face clouding over with the horrible memory. "Our friends were being murdered. The ones who weren't being murdered were in hiding or exile. The headless bodies of our students were showing up on the doorsteps of their parents."[5]

At the end of the year, a shaken Mary-Claire returned with her husband to the United States. For a year, she did post-doctoral work in epidemiology (a branch of science that deals with studying diseases) at the San Francisco campus of the University of California and in 1975 gave birth to their daughter, Emily King Colwell. In 1976 she took a job as assistant professor of epidemiology at the School of Public Health at the University of California at Berkeley.

When Emily was five, Mary-Claire divorced her husband. She said, "I was a young mother, a young scientist and a young wife. Something had to collapse, and it was the marriage."[6] By 1984 she was appointed full professor.

In June of that year, a colleague told her about an extraordinary grassroots human rights organization in Buenos Aires, Argentina, called Las Abuelas de la Plaza de Mayo [The Grandmothers of the Plaza of May]. These women were the survivors of a seven-year reign of terror that began in 1976 when Isabel Perón's civilian government was overthrown by a military coup. The upheaval resulted in the deaths of an estimated 12,000 people. Suspected opponents of the military regime would be abducted on the street and never heard from again. Pregnant women were kept alive and tortured until they gave birth, and then they were killed. Their children were either sold on the black market or given away as rewards to members of the military. These new "parents" would pretend that the children were their own, but news of what had really happened spread quickly.

In 1977, at the very start of the reign of terror, a group of grandmothers formed Las Abuelas de la Plaza de Mayo to protest the atrocities and demand the return of their grandchildren. Despite a ban against public gatherings, the old women would bravely meet outside the military regime's offices every Thursday afternoon to march.

The grandmothers questioned anyone and everyone who might know something about their missing grandchildren. Soon, others joined their crusade and would contact the grandmothers with new leads. When they saw that a baby had appeared in a family where the woman had not been pregnant, the grandmothers would be informed immediately. Teachers would tell the grandmothers whenever they encountered phony looking birth records for children enrolling in kindergarten.

By the time the military regime crumbled in 1983, the grandmothers had collected information on 144 children and had begun court cases demanding that the children be returned to their blood relatives. They realized, however, that the data might not hold up in a court of law. They needed more powerful proof.

Genetic tests had been used to identify a child's biological parents. Since most of the parents of Argentina's abducted children had been murdered, the grandmothers wondered if a similar genetic test could be used to prove that a child was related to the grandparents. In 1983 two grandmothers came to the United States to discuss this possibility with members of the American Association for the Advancement of Scientific Freedom. They were referred to Mary-Claire King.

Listening to the grandmothers' accounts, Dr. King was

horrified. In 1984 she flew to Argentina and began working eighteen-hour days to create a genetic test. Eventually she devised a test based on human leucocyte antigen (HLA) genes. These genes help manufacture proteins that stimulate the immune system's responses. By taking blood samples from a child and the supposed grandparents, she could run HLA tests to show if they shared the same gene combinations. If they did, they were almost certainly related.

The first case that King's test was used on was that of an eight-year-old girl named Paula Eva Logares. She was living with a military officer and his girlfriend, who had supposedly given birth to her. The grandmothers had amassed information indicating that the child had been abducted when she was twenty-three months old, after her parents had disappeared.

"We proved," Mary-Claire recalled, "with 99.9 percent certainty, on the basis of the HLA testing and blood groups, that Paula was a descendant of the three living grandparents who claimed her. When she went back to her grandparents' house, which she hadn't seen since she was two, she walked straight to the room where she'd slept as a baby and asked for her doll."[7]

By 1994 King's tests had helped reunite fifty children with their blood relatives and proved that an additional twelve children were not living with their biological parents, though their actual families were not found. Eventually the Argentine government established a national blood bank so that anyone who had lost a child could have a blood sample on record with the hope that one day a match would be made.

Mary-Claire said that one of the most powerful things any of the grandmothers said to her was this: "At one level," the old woman said, "we thank you very much. But at another level we are not going to thank you. Because we know that if you had been born in Buenos Aires instead of Chicago, you too would be dead, while we would be looking for your daughter."[8]

In addition to her work in Argentina, Mary-Claire used her genetic sleuthing skills to help identify the newly recovered remains of military personnel who had been listed as missing in action during the Vietnam War. She also ran genetic tests to identify the victims of a massacre by Salvadoran armed forces in 1981.

One reporter noted, "Nearly everything [Mary-Claire King] has ever chosen to work on has had, at its core, a deep sense of humanity."[9] It is this drive to help people that spurred the work for which she is best known—her research into the genetic causes of breast cancer. "The risk of breast cancer over the lifetime of an American woman is appallingly high," she said, "close to ten percent. That's equivalent to the risk of lung cancer for a heavy smoker."[10]

A goal that Mary-Claire held for many years was to try to identify the genes responsible for breast cancer. Like other cancers, breast cancer is caused when there is a mutation in the genes. Mutations can be inherited, but usually they occur later in life, either by chance or in response to carcinogens, such as viruses, radiation, or environmental toxins. Inheriting a gene that has a mutation doesn't mean that people will automatically develop cancer, but rather that they have one serious strike against them.

Scientists assumed that in some cases breast cancer was inherited because it seemed to run in certain families, and these women tended to get the disease when they were relatively young—in their thirties and forties. It seemed likely that they were inheriting a mutation in some gene that greatly increased their risk of getting cancer. Mary-Claire reasoned that this gene with the mutation might also be the same gene that caused women to develop breast cancer when no other female relative had the disease.

The trick would be finding the gene. Mary-Claire once again found that her imagination was outpacing the technology of the time. There were few tools available to help her isolate and study individual genes, and almost all of her colleagues were extremely skeptical of her project. Looking back on it, she laughed and said, "The limitation . . . should have daunted me if I'd been more sensible."[11]

But she pushed ahead and began collecting blood from 323 individuals from twenty-three families in whom breast cancer was so common they referred to it as "the family curse." Then she studied the samples, using what was then a revolutionary technique called riflip analysis.

Riflips (restriction fragment length polymorphisms) are tiny stretches of DNA that occur in the same place in everyone's chromosomes and can serve as genetic markers. King hoped that she would find a distinctive riflip marker in a woman and her relatives who had developed breast cancer. This would suggest that the breast cancer gene resided near the marker and that it was being passed down from one generation to the next.

In the early years of her research there were very few markers available. She likened her search to "driving around a foreign town at night, with only one streetlight every ten blocks, trying to locate an address."[12] But with advances in molecular biology in the mid-1980s, more markers were identified, which would equate to the streetlights in her analogy. With these molecular tools in hand, she and her research team at Berkeley continued to keep trying one marker after another to see if it was linked to the breast cancer gene. In August 1990 she tested the 183rd marker, which was from chromosome 17. It seemed as if she'd finally hit the jackpot! There was evidence showing that other women had inherited this same distinctive marker. But some of the women she tested had not. Maybe, she worried, it was only a false clue.

Then she recalled that in her earlier research she had devised a mathematical model that tracked the occurrence of breast cancer throughout the families of 1,579 women with the disease. According to her calculations, approximately 4 percent of the women were likely to have inherited a mutated gene. There were other women, however, who would seem to be from families with many victims of the disease, yet they would not have inherited a mutation. Rather, according to the mathematical model, their cancer would be a result of phenomenally bad luck—not genetics. The problem was that it seemed impossible to tell which patients belonged to which group.

Mary-Claire realized that there was a chance that the women who did not have the distinctive riflip marker in chromosome 17 might be members of the group of women identified by her mathematical model as not being inheritors of the mutated gene. But how could she be certain?

A research assistant suggested that they reorganize the families by the age of onset of breast cancer, assuming that those women who exhibited it earliest probably had inherited the disease. After that, everything fell into place. The marker was clearly inherited in the families with early onset of breast cancer. Almost certainly, somewhere on chromosome 17 was the breast cancer gene! The trick would be finding the exact gene among the thousands of possibilities.

After she announced her discovery at a meeting of geneticists, the race was on. Nobel Laureate James Watson, the co-discoverer of the structure of DNA said, "There is no greater prize in science than the long-sought master switch that may trigger breast cancer."[13] Researchers from all over the world turned their attention to chromosome 17. Soon the field narrowed even further to a region made up of about one hundred genes. Mary-Claire and her team at Berkeley worked around the clock getting closer and closer to finding the gene that was dubbed BRCA1 (for BReast CAncer 1). "We're obsessed," she admitted.[14]

In September 1994 another group of scientists, led by Mark H. Skolnick of the University of Utah Medical Center in Salt Lake City, announced that they had found BRCA1. Although disappointed that she had not found it first, Mary-Claire gracefully acknowledged their feat. "This is beautiful work, these are lovely, well-done papers, and these guys deserve their success," she said. "But it's clear that what they've found is a very complicated gene."[15]

The discovered gene is ten times larger than average, and it is unusually prone to mutation. Some of these mutations seermed more problematic than others. "Of all the sorts of genes BRCA1 might have been," Mary-Claire said, "this one is as difficult to work with as we could imagine."[16]

One out of every two hundred women was found to be a carrier of the gene. These women have an 85 percent chance of developing breast cancer and a 60 percent chance of developing ovarian cancer. For them, the discovery of the gene may mean a better shot at a long life. The sooner breast cancer is detected, the more treatable it is. Women who know they have the mutated gene can increase their surveillance so that if they do start to develop symptoms they can detect cancer early.

Mary-Claire is currently helping doctors like Susan Love, a surgeon who is at the forefront of the fight against cancer, search for more effective ways to treat the disease and hopes to "use the molecular information we can get from the gene to develop what's been called molecular mammography, a way of visualizing minute changes in breast tissue the minute they begin, rather than waiting until there's a sizable lump, as we currently do."[17]

Since the late 1980s Mary-Claire King has also been studying the possible genetic reasons why some people infected with HIV—the virus that causes AIDS—progress rapidly to full-blown AIDS while others progress more slowly.

Knowing this information could help find a drug that would fight the onset of the disease or even help in discovering a vaccine to kill the virus.

Mary-Claire King has received numerous awards, including in 1994 the most prestigious award given by the American Cancer Society for cancer research. But in many ways, her greatest rewards come from knowing that she has helped so many people through her work. She says simply, "I've always wanted to do science for the right reasons," and the knowledge that a woman with breast cancer may live longer because of the discovery of BRCA1 is proof that she has succeeded.[18]

FIVE

Mary Leakey

When we look around our modern-day world at our cars and buildings, our works of great art and literature, our complex systems of government, it seems that the gap between us and every other animal on the planet is immeasurable. Yet most scientists believe that millions of years ago our species evolved from the apes and that we share a common ancestor with chimps and gorillas and orangutans.

Ever since the theory of evolution was understood, archaeologists have searched for the fossilized remains of the "missing link," or the intermediate creature who existed between apes and humans that would complete the evolutionary sequence. Most scientists thought that humans had originiated in Asia or Europe. But the archaeological husband-and-wife team of Mary and Louis Leakey proved that Africa was actually the birthplace of humans.

Although Mary's importance was often overshadowed by her more flamboyant and theatrical husband, she was actually responsible for many of their dazzling finds. These finds

51

helped demonstrate that the lineage of apelike ancestors that led to man was far more diverse and considerably more ancient than anyone had previously imagined.

Mary Nicol was born on Feburary 6, 1913, in London, England, the only child of Erskine and Cecilia Nicol. Her father was a successful artist, and much of Mary's childhood was spent abroad traveling to the picturesque European spots that he enjoyed painting.

Mary inherited from her father a great deal of artistic ability as well as an interest in archaeology. One of Erskine's friends was Abbé Lemozi, a priest and an amateur archaeologist who had discovered ancient wallpaintings in a cave near his home in Cabrerets, France. He agreed to show the paintings to Mary, and she recalled that it was "an experience that made a really profound impression on me. . . . We had to crawl with lamps for a very long way through low and narrow passages. . . . The paintings, seen hitherto by so few eyes, were magnificent."[1] There was nothing, Mary thought, that could be more exciting than spending her life searching for clues about people who had lived so long ago. She knew she wanted to become an archaeologist.

When Mary was only thirteen her father died. Soon after, Mary's mother decided that it was time for her daughter to go to school. Until then, Mary's father had tutored her while they were abroad, but she had never attended a school and had no experience with the structure and demands of a classroom. She was quickly expelled from the first school for purposely exploding a chemistry experiment, and from the next one for filling her mouth with soap to make it appear as if she were foaming at the mouth. Her mother gave up. Never again would Mary attend school.

This did not mean that her education came to an end. She was still determined to become an archaeologist and attended lectures about prehistory at the museum and local college. In 1930 a woman archaeologist, Dorothy Liddell, offered Mary a job as her assistant. At that time Dr. Liddell was working on a number of Neolithic sites in southern Britain. Mary later said that Dr. Liddell was "an enormous help in training me, showing me how to dig properly and making it quite clear that females could go to the top of the tree."[2] One of Mary's skills that especially impressed her mentor was her talent for drawing. It was a common practice for archaeologists to make sketches of the artifacts they had found, and Mary spent many hours drawing their finds.

Her drawings soon attracted the attention of another woman archaeologist, Gertrude Caton-Thompson. For her upcoming book *The Desert Fayoum*, she asked Mary to draw some pictures of stone tools she had discovered. In 1933 she invited Mary to join her at a lecture at the Royal Anthropological Institute in London, where a successful young archaeologist named Louis Leakey would be speaking about his work in Africa.

After the lecture, Louis asked Mary to do some drawings for his book *Adam's Ancestors*. A few months later, they realized that they were falling in love. Louis, however, was married and the father of two young children. After he obtained a divorce, they were married on December 24, 1936, and a few weeks later set off together for a dig in Africa.

Louis had been born in Kenya, Africa, in 1903, the son of English missionaries who worked with the Kikuyu people of East Africa. Louis grew up speaking Kikuyu and learned the customs of the natives. He was also educated by English governesses and later went on to get a degree in anthropology from Cambridge University in England.

When he announced to his professors that he had a

hunch he would find traces of early man in Africa, they shook their heads. "Without exception," Louis recalled, "they told me it was a waste to return to Kenya. I was just being mad."[3] But two years before he met Mary, he had gone to a place called Olduvai Gorge, Tanzania, that was thought to be rich in fossils. There he had found several ancient axes. He reasoned that with so many tools, there was a good chance he would also be able to find the remains of the humanlike creatures who had made them. He hoped he'd even find the fossil remains to the "missing link."

Fossils are defined as bone or other material from once-living animals or plants that is found in the earth and maintains its form for many years. Minerals replace the original structure. Then erosion of the surrounding sediment exposes the fossils.

Fossils are very rare. Most bones are eroded, crushed, or destroyed in any number of ways. Of these surviving fossils, even a smaller number are from human ancestors. "Trying to infer the story of human history from such scattered evidence, . . ." one writer said, "is like trying to follow the story of *War and Peace* from 12 pages torn from the novel. And like *War and Peace* the story of mankind is long."[4]

Louis was certain that a number of important "pages" might be hiding in Olduvai, but he could not get funding for such a dig. Soon after marrying Mary, however, he managed to win a two-year scholarship to study the Kikuyu people in Nakuru, Kenya. Nearby were two other important archaeological sites he had worked on earlier—Hyrax Hill and the Njoro River Cave. The latter had been used as a Late Stone Age cremation ground around 850 B.C. It was decided that while Louis gathered research for his project, Mary would excavate the sites.

Their home was a tiny grass *banda*, or thatched hut. However, they had a beautiful view of golden fields and, in the distance, a sparkling lake. Often the shores would be crowded with thousands of bright flamingos.

Mary fell in love with the archaeological sites. All day she would sift through the dirt searching for tools, bead necklaces, and drinking vessels. At night, she would return home to study and classify her finds.

On November 4, 1940, the couple's first child, Johnathan Harry Erskine Leakey, was born. "I quite like[d] having a baby . . . ," Mary Leakey said, "but I had no intention of allowing motherhood to disrupt my work as an archaeologist."[5]

She would take Johnathan along with her on the digs, leaving him in the shade while she worked. In 1942 she gave birth to their second child, daughter Deborah, who died from dysentery when she was only three months old. In 1944 Richard was born.

During this time, World War II was raging in Europe, and Africa was subject to gas rationing. Mary used the gas she could acquire to travel to various sites, including Olorgesailie in the Kenya Rift Valley, where she uncovered thousands of hand axes and cleavers from the late Paleolithic period (which lasted from about 2.5 million to about 10,000 years ago). Most of these artifacts were left in place, and the site has become a major tourist attraction.

After the war, Louis took over a post as the curator of the Coryndon Museum in Nairobi. He and Mary began planning the first Pan-African Congress of Prehistory and Paleontology. The conference was a tremendous success, with the Leakeys taking eminent archaeologists from all over the world to visit their African excavations. The Leakeys also managed to obtain funds to work on an expedition to Rusinga Island in Tanzania's Lake Victoria.

Louis had first visited the island in 1926 and determined then that it might be a good place to find fossils from the Miocene Period (the geologic period dating from approximately 25 million years ago to 5 million years ago). In 1942 he had found the jawbone of an ancient extinct ape on the island and hoped to do more research there. The funds now gave them this chance.

They began by excavating an astounding array of new mammals at Rusinga, including ancient pigs, elephants, apes, and rhinos. One writer compared the island to "a fossilized ark, bearing with it all the forms of life that had once roamed its shores," except any humanlike creature that may have been one of our ancient ancestors.[6] The Leakeys kept turning up animal bones, but nothing human. What they didn't know was that the most exciting discovery was still to come.

"Awaiting me . . . ," Mary Leakey later wrote, "where it had lain for about 18 million years, was one of the most spectacular discoveries of my entire life."[7]

On October 6, 1948, she had been examining a stretch of interesting sloping earth when her eyes wandered upward and spotted a tooth embedded in the sediment. It looked almost human! Her heart racing, she began brushing away the sediment with a fine brush, and then used a dental pick to gently scrape away more earth. She called for Louis, and as they worked together, they realized the find was humanlike, and not only was there a tooth, but also a jaw and an entire skull in fragments. She had found the first skull of an extinct primitive ape known as *proconsul africanus.*

While Louis telegraphed the West with news of the discovery, Mary (who was pregnant with their last child, Philip) spent long hours fitting together the thirty or more pieces of the skull. When she had finally reconstructed the skull, it was decided that Mary would take it back to London to show the world what she had found.

She put the skull in a biscuit tin lined with cotton and boarded the plane. By the time she arrived in London, newspapers had already started printing stories about the remarkable discovery. As she stepped into the airport, she was inundated by reporters and photographers. Until this point, Mary had been seen as existing in her husband's shadow, but now it was clear that she was a talented archaeologist in her own right.

The skull helped prove what Louis had long believed—that East Africa might be the cradle of mankind. On a practical level, it brought more attention and increased funding to the Leakeys' work. This included money for them to work at the site in Olduvai, Tanzania, that Louis had long thought would be profitable. Fossils had originally been discovered at this site by an entomologist (a scientist who studies insects). He was chasing a butterfly and fell into a gorge. Lying on the ground, he noticed numerous fossils embedded in the dry earth.

Olduvai was in the largely uninhabited territory known as the Serengeti Plains. Wild animals—lions, leopards, elephants, and zebras—roamed the vast grassy lands. Here the Leakeys kept their own menagerie of unusual pets, including wildebeest calves, orphaned antelopes, and a group of black-and-white spotted dalmatian dogs.

Although a beautiful and dramatic landscape, it was a rough place to live. Fine black dust blew constantly, and far away from civilization, the Leakeys often ran out of supplies. During the dry season, water was very scarce. Ponds became filthy wallows that the local rhinos liked to roll in. As Mary said, "Our soup, tea, or coffee all tasted of rhino urine, which we never quite got used to."[8]

Mary and Louis uncovered numerous fossils in Olduvai, including the bones of giraffes that were twice as tall as modern-day ones, with giant thick horns like moose antlers. But they found no traces of the human ancestors who may have hunted the creatures.

Then, on July 17, 1959, Mary went out for a walk with her group of dogs. As always, she walked bent forward, staring at the earth, eyes scanning for telltale hints of fossils. Suddenly she noticed a bit of bone. It seemed to be part of a skull. Until this time, she and Louis had found numerous interesting fossils, but none of a human. She bent down, dusted away earth, and saw fossilized teeth and the bone of a jaw. She built a little pile of stones to mark the spot, then raced back to Louis, who had been feeling ill and was lying in bed at the house.

"I've got him! I've got him! I've got him!" she shouted.[9] Ignoring his illness, Louis jumped out of bed and raced after her. That afternoon they did not begin excavation on the skull because, ironically, a film crew was due to arrive to document some of their work. Louis realized that this would make for wonderful drama. So he convinced Mary to wait until the crew arrived.

The film of the excavation was shown on television back in England and captured the public's imagination. Viewers felt as if they were witnessing a great discovery and could share the feeling that Louis later described as "sheer joy. . . . After all our hoping and hardship and sacrifice, at last we had reached our goal—we had discovered the world's earliest known human."[10]

Mary wondered if she had found the long-sought missing link. It would turn out that this 1.75-million-year-old creature, named *Zinjanthropus boisei*, or "Zinj," was a type of prehuman called a "hominid." It was not a direct ancestor of modern humans, and it eventually became extinct. It did, however, exist at approximately the same time as the missing-link hominids. Zinj and other discoveries by the Leakeys would prove that there was more than one type of hominid living at the same time in the same area—something scientists had not believed possible.

Once again, Mary boarded a plane with her find in a biscuit tin. Reporters dubbed Zinj the "Nutcracker Man" because of his huge back molars. The public, having witnessed Zinj's discovery on television, was thrilled with the arrival of the skull and its finder. The National Geographic Society decided to begin funding the Leakeys' work on a much larger scale. They were becoming heroes in America as well as in England.

When Mary returned to Africa, she continued to work mainly at Olduvai while Louis spent more and more time abroad, traveling, raising funds, and delighting huge audiences with his lectures. Mary's prominence faded in comparsion to her husband's worldwide fame and popularity.

After 1968 the Leakeys were rarely together. Their marriage, which Mary had described as an "idyllic partnership," had deteriorated.[11] Louis's health was failing, and in 1972 he died from a heart attack.

Mary continued working at Olduvai and in 1974 led a team of researchers in excavations at Laetoli, Tanzania, about thirty miles away. There they found fossil remains of ancient humans 3.6 to 3.8 million years old, the oldest fossils yet discovered. On the basis of these finds, Mary received a large grant from the National Geographic Society to continue work at Laetoli.

In 1976 a couple of the men on her research team were horsing around. One man threw a clump of elephant dung at his friend. The other man ducked and knelt on the ground. Looking down, he noticed interesting ridges in the dry, hard earth. Dusting a bit of soil away, he saw what appeared to be an ancient footprint! Mary came over to look. It did resemble an ancient human print. What they discovered would stun the world and give modern humans a rare insight into life millions of years ago.

Imagine this scenario: A local volcano has been erupting for weeks. Fine volcanic ash settles over the land and when the rains come, this ash becomes soft and doughy. As the animals of the area dash by, they leave behind their footprints. Also three creatures—who from a distance might look like a family of apes, but are hairless—walk through the muck. The sun bakes their prints into the wet, ashy earth, to remain unnoticed for 3.5 million years, until a researcher ducked to avoid a clump of elephant dung!

Upon excavation, Mary's team discovered that the footprints stretched for eighty or more feet. It was, she recalled, "immensely exciting—something so extraordinary that I could hardly take it in or comprehend its implications for some while."[12] Until this time, scientists had been arguing about when man's ancestors began walking in a fully upright position. It was assumed that this question could never be definitively answered. But the Laetoli prints demonstrated beyond a doubt, that our ancestors were "bipedal" (walking fully upright) 3.5 million years ago. The discovery was one of the most important in all of archaeology.

After numerous researchers came to study the prints, Mary Leakey reburied them to protect them from erosion and damage by wild animals. Recently, however, scientists have become worried about a grove of trees that has gradually encroached on the area, sending down roots that threaten to break up the prints. In 1995 the Getty Institute of Southern California paid to have the trees removed and to perform conservation measures on the footprints.

In 1980 Mary decided to return to Olduvai and continued excavating. Two years later, she woke up one morning to find she had lost the sight in her left eye. Doctors told her that this was caused by a blood clot. She decided to pass the care of Olduvai to the Tanzanian Department of Antiquities and moved to Nairobi. Here she worked on her autobiography, *Disclosing the Past*, which was published two years later to much popular acclaim. She continued her field research as much as possible despite her loss of vision.

She has been given a number of important awards for her work, and the woman who had never attended school was honored with degrees from several universities, including Yale and Oxford.

Her son Johnathan married and settled in Kenya to raise snakes and melons. The youngest son, Philip, became the first white official in the Kenyan government. And Richard, after becoming a noted archaeologist in his own right, emerged as one of the leading wildlife conservationists, campaigning for a global ban on ivory sales to try to end the poaching of elephants.

Mary Leakey died in early December 1996. She was eighty-three years old.

SIX

~

RITA
LEVI-MONTALCINI

Rita Levi-Montalcini was reading a mystery novel by Agatha Christie when the phone rang in her apartment in Rome with the news that she had won the Nobel Prize for physiology and medicine. "I was very happy about it," she laughed, "but I wanted much more to know the end of the story."[1]

In many ways, Rita's own life and career are as full of exciting plot twists as a good mystery novel. She began her medical career at the same time that Hitler's armies were invading her native Italy. A Jew, Rita went into hiding and decided to set up a secret laboratory in the cramped confines of her bedroom. Here she began experiments that would one day lead her to make the groundbreaking discovery of nerve growth factor, for which she was awarded the Nobel Prize in 1986. "If I had not been discriminated against or had not suffered persecution," she wryly declared, "I would never have received the Nobel Prize."[2]

~

Rita and her unidentical twin sister, Paola, were born on April 22, 1909, in Turin, Italy. They had three older siblings but felt like soulmates to each other.

Adamo Levi, Rita's father, was an engineer who ran a factory for ice and the distilling of alcohol. He made all important decisions for the family. His "imperious voice which contrasted so sharply with the sweetness of my mother's not only pointed to differences in their personalities but offered me the first tangible evidence of just how different were the roles of men and women in the society of the day," she said.[3]

Her father decided that although Rita and her sister showed an outstanding aptitude for study they should go to a girls' high school where they would learn only enough to prepare them to become mothers and wives.

Paola was not troubled by the realization that she would never get a college degree because she had already decided she would be an artist. But Rita said that even when young she knew she "was not cut out to be a wife. Babies did not attract me, and I was altogether without the maternal sense."[4] What would she do with her life if she did not marry?

It was not until she was twenty that she found her direction. Rita had gone to pay her last respects to a beloved servant named Giovanna, who was dying of stomach cancer. Clasping the woman's frail hand in her own, Rita vowed to find a way to help people like Giovanna by going into medicine.

When she told her father of her dream, he tried to discourage her, but Rita's mind was made up. Finally he gave her permission to hire a tutor to help her try to catch up on all the information she would need to pass the medical school's admissions exam. When she finally took the test in 1930, Rita earned the highest score of any candidate.

After passing her first year of medical school with honors, she became an intern at the Institute of Anatomy where she worked with the brilliant scientist Giuseppe Levi (no relation).

He would become a lifelong friend, as well as an adviser and colleague. At first, however, their relationship was rocky.

He had assigned Rita to the task of determining how the convolutions of the human brain are formed. For her research, she needed to find human fetuses (that had been miscarried) to dissect, but this was virtually impossible. At one point a hospital worker offered her the corpse of a newborn infant. Although not as useful as a fetus, she decided to examine it nonetheless. While she was riding the streetcar, the child's leg fell out of the bundle she had wrapped it in. Fortunately, none of the other passengers noticed.

Rita decided that the project was a waste of time and convinced Levi to allow her to abandon it. "It was a stupid question," she said later, "which I couldn't solve and no one could solve."[5] She then began to study the development of the nervous system in chick embryos. It would be her first foray into what at that time was the very new field of neurology [the science of the nervous system].

Until the end of the nineteenth century, most scientists thought that the nervous system could not be subject to examination. They felt that the laws of biology that governed other biological processes, such as breathing or digestion, could not apply to that mysterious organ, the brain. But shortly after the turn of the century, scientists had shown that the nervous system was made up of cells like all other parts of the body and that they seemed to be governed by similar biological and physical laws. One question that then intrigued researchers was how does a single fertilized cell grow and develop into an organism as complex as the human body? Rita's work went to the heart of this question. She wanted to know how something as complex as our nervous system develops in an embryo.

It had been shown that the development of the nervous system in chick embryos was roughly identical to that in all other vertebrates, including humans. Rita hoped that by studying development in chicks, she could learn things about the development of the nervous system in humans.

This course of study greatly excited her, but her happiness was tempered in 1932 by the death of her father. Over the years, Rita had gradually grown to admire his passion, his stubbornness, and his intellect. She regretted that there had been so much distance between them during her childhood.

In 1936 she graduated from medical school with top honors and began a three-year postgraduate course in neurology and psychiatry. She continued her studies of chick embryos and worked at the university's medical clinic, caring for the poor. Sometimes she thought she would like to continue on as a doctor; at other times, she was drawn to the world of research.

At this time, Hitler's armies were gathering force, and the Nazis' anti-Semitic campaigns were terrorizing Jews. In 1938 Benito Mussolini, the head of Italy's Fascist government, issued a decree that, among other things, banned Jews from all university positions and forbade them from practicing medicine. While Mussolini did not personally harbor particular hatred of Jews, he ordered the decree to curry favor with Hitler.

Rita continued to work at the university in an atmosphere of growing hostility. Newspaper articles were filled with anti-Semitic propaganda. She was horrified to discover that the study of eugenics (science that deals with the improvement of hereditary qualities of a race or breed) was becoming fashionable as a perverse way of trying to establish the supremacy of the so-called Aryan race. (Aryans, the Fascists claimed, were white gentiles.) She was sickened by reading supposedly "scientific" reports by researchers who were attempting to prove that there was a risk involved in the marriage of an Aryan and a Jew. They claimed to have data proving, for example, that grave difficulties could arise "if . . . the offspring of any such marriage inherited the strong skeleton of the Aryan father and the frail organs of the Jewish mother."[6]

By March of 1939 Rita was ready to leave her troubled

country and accepted an invitation to continue her work in Belgium. When she returned to Turin in December of that year, the Nazis had invaded Poland and World War II had started. Rita began to work secretly as a doctor caring for the poor but was forced to quit when it became impossible for her, as a Jew, to get prescriptions filled.

At the suggestion of a friend, Rita decided to set up a makeshift laboratory in her bedroom so that she could continue the studies of chicken embryos. Equipment was hard to come by, but she managed to craft most of her tools herself. She used a grindstone to sharpen sewing needles into sharp scalpels and her brother helped her to transform common thermostats into incubators for the eggs. These eggs were in scarce supply during the war, so when she would visit local farmers she would tell them that she needed the eggs to feed her hungry children. Few farmers could resist such a heartfelt plea. To assuage her guilt for lying, she would take the eggs into the kitchen after she had finished working with them and cook the yolks into omelets. The one piece of equipment she was forced to buy was an expensive microscope.

During this time, Rita decided to ask her old mentor, Giuseppe Levi, if he would be interested in helping her with the research. As a Jew, he too had been banished from the university and accepted her offer. Rita laughed, "with his great corporeal mass [body size] and meager agility, he threatened to destroy all the carefully laid out [microscope slides]."[7]

An even greater threat to the lab was from bombs. Hitler's armies were marching across Europe and on to Russia. The Allies were regularly bombing Turin, and night after night the air-raid sirens would sound. Every time they did, Rita would grab her valuable microscope and head with her family and Giuseppe down into their basement bomb shelter.

Her work consisted of using her homemade scalpels to cut the limbs off chicken embryos. In a healthy embryo, nerve cells develop in the spinal cord and then move out to the

67

limb. But Rita wanted to know what would happen to the nerve cells in the spinal cord if that limb were cut off. Would they continue to develop? Or would they somehow realize that the limb was no longer there and not develop?

Similar experiments had been done by a researcher named Viktor Hamburger at Washington University in St. Louis, Missouri. Rita had read his reports and knew that he had found that a week after an embryo's limb was cut the nerve cells destined for that spot would die. If another limb was grafted on, the nerve cells would flourish. He concluded that there must be something in the limb that tells the cells in the spinal cord to develop, or "differentiate," and move out. When the limb is gone, the cells have nothing to tell them to differentiate and move out, so they don't.

After careful study of embryos with cut-off limbs, Rita reached a different conclusion. She had noticed that the cells in the spinal area did differentiate even without the limb. In fact, they differentiated in the same way as they did in normal embryos. However, in those embryos without limbs, the cells eventually died. Rita concluded that the limb did not tell the cells to differentiate as Hamburger thought, but rather it provided them with some kind of nutrient needed for the differentiated nerve's survival. Without the limb there was no nutrient, and so these differentiated cells died. No Italian scientific journal would publish her findings because she was a Jew, but a publisher in Belgium agreed to print her piece.

Rita's research was cut short in September of 1943 when the Nazis took over northern Italy. Rita and her family knew they were in great danger and decided to flee. Without any clear plan in mind, they boarded a southward-bound train, hoping to evade the advancing Germans. They got off in Florence and found an apartment.

The landlady said that she could not risk renting to Jews and asked them their religion. They said they were Catholics and gave fake names. Their true identity was revealed when

Giuseppe Levi arrived at the door one afternoon and asked the landlady, "Do you have a Rita Levi—I mean, Lupani—living here?"[8] Fortunately the landlady had already figured out that Rita's family were Jews and had made the risky decision to continue to allow them to live in her home.

On November 2, 1944, British troops marched through Florence, freeing the city. The war was effectively over, but the people were still in danger. A typhoid epidemic broke out, and Rita nursed the sick, ignoring the threat to her own life.

Soon, however, Rita received an offer from Viktor Hamburger to come to the United States and work with him in St. Louis. He had read in the Belgium journal her analysis of the experiments she had done repeating his own studies of chick embryos, and he was intrigued by her conclusions. At the time, Rita had started to have doubts about the usefulness of her work in embryology but could not pass up the opportunity to visit America. So she boarded the ship, waved goodbye to her beloved family, and set sail.

Dr. Hamburger was so impressed with her experiments that he asked her to stay longer than originally planned. Still, she continued to have grave doubts about the usefulness of the work, but this changed when, in 1950, Dr. Hamburger showed her an interesting article by one of his talented former students, Elmer Bueker. Bueker had found that if he grafted a cancerous tumor from a mouse onto a chick embryo, nerve fibers would invade the tumor and then grow very rapidly inside of it. He concluded that the tumor must create a rich environment for the nerve cells.

But Rita suspected there was a more important message in this experiment, "whose meaning it was up to us to discover."[9] Often in science, it is at such a moment when a researcher finds a fresh way of looking at a result that the greatest advances are made. Convinced that there was more to learn, Rita asked Bueker for his permission to continue his experiments and then ordered a box of mice infected with this particular cancerous tumor. Repeating his experiment, Rita watched in amazement as nerve fibers grew rapidly not only in the tumor but also in other organs, including the spleen, thyroid, and liver. She thought the tumors must be releasing a chemical that was speeding up the growth of nerve cells. This chemical would later be called nerve growth factor (NGF).

When she discussed her theory with Giuseppe Levi, he was dismissive. It seemed too far-fetched. Tumor chemicals that could make nerves grow? He told her she would embarrass herself if she published her theory. This only spurred Rita to devise an experiment that would prove there was some sort of chemical inside the tumor that was speeding up nerve growth. After much thought, she "took a glass dish and placed in it a nerve ganglion [a group of nerve cells] with a tumor nearby [but not touching]. If the nerve fibers sprang out from the ganglion in the dish, surely no one would then doubt that a fluid . . . was at work."[10] The experiment worked!

Viktor Hamburger knew she had discovered something very important about how nerves grow. He arranged for her to work with a young, talented biochemist named Stanley Cohen, who would help Rita determine the makeup of the chemical in the tumor. They were an odd pair. Rita was always meticulously attired in her Italian-style chic suits, while Stanley was always rumpled, wearing mismatched socks and scruffy shoes. He had a mutt that followed him everywhere. As scientists, however, they were a perfect match.

By the end of the year, Stan was certain the NGF was a protein. And then, the two researchers discovered that the same factor was also present in snake venom and mouse salivary glands. It was easier to extract large amounts of the factor from these two new sources than from mouse tumors. Soon, Stan was able to develop an antifactor out of the antidote to snake venom that would slow nerve growth. He also identified another growth factor that he named epidermal growth factor, which was found to stimulate many processes in humans, including the growth of cells in the skin, immune system, blood, and liver.

But then in December of 1958, Viktor Hamburger had some bad news. Budget cuts meant that Washington University would be unable to offer Stan Cohen a full-time faculty position. The fruitful partnership was forced to come to an end. In the spring of 1961 Rita returned to Rome to be nearer her family and to set up the Laboratory of Cell Biology. She continued to visit Washington University, but the following years were filled with frustration.

The news of NGF had spread all over the world, and researchers were intent on learning more about its possible uses. Rita, however, was rarely acknowledged as its discoverer. When she attended conferences on the subject, few people knew who she was. And, she said, "My name was entirely left out of the literature. . . . I am not a person to be bitter, but it was astonishing to find it completely canceled."[11]

Whether or not the scientific community acknowledged her, Rita could not deny that the research being done was exciting. Much of this work continues today in labs worldwide. Scientists are searching for ways to use NGF to help repair the damage caused to nerves by degenerative diseases such as Huntington's chorea, Parkinson's, and Alzheimer's. Other researchers are hoping to find a way to use an antifactor to prohibit the growth of cancerous cells and tumors.

In 1986 Rita finally was guaranteed that she would receive the credit she deserved for her discovery. The Nobel Prize was awarded to her and Stanley Cohen.

Although Rita Levi-Montalcini is now in her eighties, she continues to work at her lab on possible uses of NGF in the immune and endocrine systems. NGF, she has said, "was just the tip of the iceberg. Even now I am doing something . . . in the same spirit as when I was a young person. And this is very pleasing to me. I mean at my old age, I could have no more capacity. And I believe I still have plenty."[12]

SEVEN

SUSAN LOVE

From far away, the hill looked as if it were covered by grave markers. In fact, they were 1,300 plaster casts of women's torsos. The Los Angeles Breast Cancer Coalition had set up the display in 1994 as a memorial to women who had died from the disease. Dr. Susan Love, an influential surgeon on the front lines fighting the war against breast cancer, watched her young daughter walk among the casts and reaffirmed her passionate commitment to do everything she could to find a cure. She has said that it is her goal to make certain that "my daughter won't be able to follow in my footsteps, because there won't be enough breast cancer for her to treat."[1]

The eldest of five children, Susan Love was born in Little Silver, New Jersey, on February 9, 1948. Her father, James Love, was a salesman for a machinery company. When Susan was thirteen, he was transferred and the family moved to Puerto

Rico. Later they moved to Mexico City, where Susan graduated from high school.

She began the pre-med program at Notre Dame of Maryland in Baltimore. After two years, however, she changed her mind and decided that she wanted to become a nun. She had been raised to believe that she should do good work for others and felt as a nun she would have a chance to help the needy. At the age of twenty she entered a convent but quickly found the life far more restraining than she had ever imagined. Five months later she left the convent to continue her college education at Fordham University in New York City. After graduating with a bachelor of science degree, she decided to pursue a medical degree. At that time, most medical schools had quotas limiting the number of women in their programs to 10 percent. Susan was thrilled to learn she had been accepted to the program at State University of New York, Downstate Medical Center, in Brooklyn. In 1974 she graduated fourth in her class.

The specialty that appealed to her was surgery, although she recognized that it was "the most male of medical specialties and the least friendly to women."[2] Surgical training was extremely rigorous, demanding five years of being on call every other night. Surgeons also tended to work long hours because of medical emergencies.

Young women interested in entering the field were routinely questioned about their plans for getting married and having children. The assumption was that if they decided to raise families, they would not be able to work such long hours and the years of training would be wasted on them. Male students were not asked similar questions because it was taken for granted that their wives would shoulder the burden of child-rearing. According to the American Medical Association, although the number of women in both general surgery and surgical specialties grew from 2,129 in 1970 to 9,733 in 1985, by 1985 still only 8 percent of all surgeons were female.[3]

Susan said that the program she entered at Beth Israel Hospital in Boston was modeled after the military. Often she'd go to work after sleeping only a few hours, but she was determined not to show any weakness and would force herself to keep concentrating long after exhaustion had set in.

By the time she completed her residency in 1979, she had been promoted to chief resident, a position highly unusual for a woman. The next year she became the first female general surgeon on staff at Beth Israel Hospital. At first she was determined not to be "ghettoized in a woman's specialty."[4] She wanted to prove "I could do the big operations just as well as [the men] could."[5] But she realized that women were consistently coming to her with breast problems.

She said, "For any other form of surgery, they might have chosen, even preferred, a male doctor—but for their breasts, they wanted someone they instinctively felt would understand their bodies and respect the particular meaning their breasts had for them."[6]

Dr. Love realized that many women feel their breasts are intimately linked with their sense of femaleness and their sexuality. Breasts are also the means by which a woman can feed her baby, and for some women they become an important part of their identity as mothers and nurturers.

It is not surprising then that many women experience a swirl of emotions when they learn they have breast cancer. By understanding and anticipating this reaction, Dr. Love quickly endeared herself to many of her patients. For example, one afternoon when an anxious patient asked, "You'll take care of me?" Dr. Love looked her in the eye and promised, "I will take good care of you."[7] Then she gave her a huge hug. Another patient recalled that as she went into surgery, Dr. Love "was holding my hand and . . . I thought 'What could be better?'"[8]

Breast cancer currently affects one out of every eight women in America. Every four minutes a woman is diagnosed with breast cancer, and every twelve minutes a woman dies of it. The sooner the cancer is detected, the better the chances of successful treatment. Usually a woman discovers that she has breast cancer when she feels a lump in her breast. Often these lumps are not problematic, but other times they are cancerous tumors that must be treated. The primary means of fighting the disease are surgery, radiation, and chemotherapy, or a combination of some of these.

Numerous surveys have shown that even though heart disease and lung cancer kill more American women than any other disease, breast cancer is the disease that women fear the most.[9] Dr. Love has said she has found that for most women "the most frightening thing [about breast problems] is not knowing, not understanding what's happening to one's own body."[10] She feels it is important for physicians to make certain that their patients receive all relevant information so they can make educated choices about their own treatments.

The more women with breast cancer that Dr. Love saw, however, the more she believed that "women weren't getting information. If they came in with a lump or what they thought was a lump, the doctor would say, 'Don't worry your little head about that, dear.'" Dr. Love said, "I realized I could make a contribution in this area."[11]

In 1981 she joined the Breast Evaluation Clinic of the Dana Farber Cancer Institute in Boston. A year later she published a groundbreaking paper in the October 1982 issue of *The New England Journal of Medicine* criticizing the frequently made diagnosis of fibrocystic disease of the breast. Dr. Love had found that doctors were routinely assigning this diagnosis to a number of different symptoms, including everything from painful breasts to lumpy breasts. In her no-nonsense style she wrote, "'Fibrocystic disease' is as fanciful as anything Lewis Carroll [the author of *Alice in Wonderland*] ever invented."[12]

Most troubling were the studies that had linked the so-called fibrocystic disease to later occurrences of breast cancer. Studying the data, Dr. Love realized that almost all of the articles were based on the same small study and that the links to breast cancer were very shaky. With the publication of her paper, Dr. Love dispelled the anxiety that many women felt who had been diagnosed with fibrocystic breasts and assumed they would one day get breast cancer as a result.

In 1987 Susan Love was appointed an assistant clinical professor in surgery at Harvard Medical School in Boston. This position allowed her to work with future physicians and to try to influence the way they treated their patients.

A good doctor, she would tell her students, is able not only to make accurate diagnoses and initiate appropriate treatments but also to empathize with patients and listen to their concerns. "Unfortunately," she said, "the medical profession hasn't done a good job of preparing doctors to work [this] way—we were all taught to say, 'if I were you, I'd do such and such,' or 'if you were my wife, I'd want you to do such and such,' which is problematic, because the patient is not us, and she's not our wife, either. Often the result is that the values of a white, middle-aged man are imposed on a patient who is female and maybe older or younger, maybe white and maybe not."[13]

In 1988 Dr. Love established Boston's Faulkner Breast Centre. This facility was the only one in the country with five women surgeons specializing in breast disease. The Centre also employed plastic surgeons specializing in breast reconstruction, radiotherapists, and other medical support staff who were all women. Dr. Love set up a data bank for research on breast problems and started a one-year fellowship for surgeons interested in developing expertise in breast surgery. She also spent her days rushing from one patient to the next, never hesitating to spend the time necessary to explain what was happening in their breasts and what they could expect in the future. On her lab coat she wore numerous cheery buttons, including ones reading "Keep Abreast," "Get a Second Opinion," and "T.G.I.F." (Thank God I'm Female).

During her tenure at Faulkner, she challenged the tendency of many surgeons to perform radical mastectomies (surgery in which the entire breast is removed) instead of more conservative lumpectomies (in which only the cancerous lump is removed). Years of research had shown that in most cases lumpectomies were as effective as mastectomies for treating cancer, and yet most women were still undergoing mastectomies. In fact, the number of women undergoing lumpectomies ranged from only 20.6 percent in the part of the country encompassing Kentucky, Tennessee, Mississippi, and Alabama to 55.1 percent in New England.[14] Dr. Love said, "Using a mastectomy to treat a [small] lesion . . . is like using a cannon to shoot a flea."[15]

She believed there were a number of indefensible reasons why surgeons were still performing so many mastectomies. For one thing, some doctors were more comfortable doing mastectomies because this was what they had been trained to do in college. Some even suggested that their patients with noncancerous breasts undergo preventive mastectomies so that they would not develop problems later. She was outraged to discover that one prominent surgeon wrote in a medical journal that he believed in "tossing the excess baggage overboard to keep the ship of life afloat."[16] The excess baggage he was referring to was a woman's breasts.

Dr. Love did not hesitate to publicly attack such patronizing attitudes. "[She] constantly challenges dogma," said one colleague. "Surgeons aren't supposed to do that. Susan makes many surgeons uncomfortable."[17]

While at Faulkner, she also began working on *Dr. Susan Love's Breast Care Book*, which was published in 1990. She saw it as another way to give women all over the country the information they needed. The book is written in a down-to-earth style and begins by discussing normal breast development, then moves on to explaining the causes of breast cancer and the various treatment options. Again and again, she urges women not to panic upon learning that they have cancer.

"The typical notion," Dr. Love has said, "is that you're a time bomb and the cancer is going to take over your body unless you do something tomorrow. Well, that's just not true."[18] Taking time to learn your options, to get a second opinion, and to decide how to proceed, she tells readers, will not make any notable difference.

In her book, Dr. Love also took what was then considered a radical step of criticizing the popular assumption that breast self-exams will help women detect cancerous lumps. She wrote, "I think it alienates women from their breasts instead of making them more comfortable with them. It puts you in a position of examining yourself once a month to see if your breast has betrayed you. It becomes you against your breast: Can you find the tiniest lump that may be cancer?"[19] Reasearch indicated that most women do not discover problematic lumps doing breast self-exams. Rather, they find the lump naturally, when turning over in bed or soaping in a shower. Instead of self-exams, she advocates that women learn to get to know their bodies, including their breasts, because "there is a powerful feeling that comes from knowing and being comfortable with your body—a feeling and a power that is yours alone, and that no one can take from you."[20]

The book was an immediate success and became a national best-seller. Dr. Love went on a book tour and began talking to women all over the country. She discovered that women from every walk of life were angry about the lack of attention paid to breast cancer. They were ready to do something to help focus the spotlight on the illness and increase funding for research into better treatments.

In June of 1990, at a talk in Salt Lake City, Dr. Love joked that maybe the only way to get Washington to wake up to the problem of breast cancer was to have women march topless on the White House. Afterward, women rushed up to her, asking how they could join the march. At that moment, Dr. Love realized that women needed a national organization to rally around and decided to found one. With the help of leaders from various political activist groups as well as a number of leading health organizations, including the American Cancer Society and breast cancer support groups, she helped found the National Breast Cancer Coalition in 1990.

One of the group's first actions was to determine ideally how much money needed to be spent on breast cancer research in the future. The coalition talked with top researchers in the field and put together a federal funding budget for 1993 of $433 million. This was $340 million more than had been spent in the previous year, and although the task seemed daunting, Dr. Love and the coalition began to lobby Congress for additional funds.

They succeeded in raising $420 million. This was due in part, Dr. Love felt, to Anita Hill, who had appeared before a Senate committee considering the appointment of Clarence Thomas to the Supreme Court and charged him with sexual harrassment. "After that debacle," she said, "congressmen were all looking for a nice, noncontroversial *women's* issue."[21]

In 1992 Dr. Love decided to leave Boston's Faulkner Hospital and take over as the director of the Breast Center at the University of California at Los Angeles (UCLA). The decision was a difficult one, but she felt that "women doctors need to bring their perspective into the medical mainstream."[22] At UCLA she would not only have an opportunity to treat patients and work with the students in the university's large medical school but also have the funding necessary to set up a research center.

Dr. Love is convinced that research is the key to winning the war on breast cancer. "It's clear," she's said, "that [the current ways of treating cancer through] surgery, radiation, and chemotherapy—'slash, burn, and poison,' as I've been known to call them—are rather crude ways of dealing with the problem."[23] The more promising hope for the future is research into the genetic causes of breast cancer.

In 1994 scientists managed to isolate a gene identified as BRCA1 that is inherited and predisposes women to early-onset breast cancer. Although this gene affects only about 4 to 5 percent of women, Dr. Love hopes that in the near future, researchers will find a way to devise tests (such as blood analysis) that will indicate when genes first start to change in an abnormal way. Such tests would allow doctors to treat patients before they develop cancer and would make the "slash, burn, and poison" treatments of today outmoded.

Most of Dr. Love's recent research has been concerned with developing a technique called Ductoscopy, which involves inserting a small scope through a nipple into a milk duct to examine tissue inside the milk ducts for suspicious cell changes. This is where most breast cancer starts. She has also been studying possible preventive uses of Tamoxifen, a drug that blocks estrogen and has been used to treat women with breast cancer.

Since 1981 Susan Love has been in a relationship with a fellow surgeon, Dr. Helen Cooksey. Dr. Love became pregnant using donated sperm, and in 1989 gave birth to a daughter, Katie. On September 10, 1993, Dr. Love and Dr. Cooksey won a landmark case allowing Cooksey to be legally recognized as Katie's co-parent.

In 1996 Dr. Love decided to retire from surgery stating, "I have been caring for patients for almost twenty years and personally feel the need for a break in order to pursue other activities."[24] She continues to work as a researcher at the UCLA Breast Center and is writing a new book about hormone replacement therapy for treating menopausal women. In her free time she has said that she wants "to take piano lessons. If I'm not going to be operating, I might as well do something with my fingers."[25]

EIGHT

Helen Taussig

The baby had a bluish tinge to her skin because of a defect in her circulatory system. She was not getting enough oxygen, and her condition was worsening. Unless something could be done, she would certainly die. Dr. Helen Taussig had developed an idea for a revolutionary type of surgery that just might save the baby's life, but no surgeon had ever tried it. Nor had any surgeon ever dared to operate on someone as small or as weak as this baby. But it became clear that if nothing were done, the baby would surely die. The desperate parents knew that Dr. Taussig's plan was their baby's only hope for life, and they gave permission to have the surgery performed.

On November 29, 1944, the child underwent the innovative operation. She survived, but died sometime later of other complications. The surgery, however, was considered a success and would eventually save the lives of countless other "blue babies." It would also encourage more doctors to explore what was then the very risky field of cardiac (heart) surgery. Dr. Taussig said that once surgeons realized a successful heart operation could be performed on small children, "they felt they could operate on almost anyone."[1]

Helen Taussig was born on May 24, 1898, in Cambridge, Massachusetts, the fourth child of Edith and Frank Taussig. When Helen was only eleven years old, her mother died from tuberculosis. Afterwards, she became even closer to her father, a respected economics professor at Harvard University. He was very kind and supportive to his daughter, who, although bright, had difficulty with reading. No matter how hard she concentrated, the letters seemed to jump around or switch order on the page. What neither Helen nor her teachers knew at that time was that she was suffering from a learning disability called dyslexia.

Helen would come running home from school, certain that she was a failure because of her inability to read. Her kind father would reassure her that she was smart in other ways. By the time Helen was ready to graduate from high school, she had learned to concentrate doubly hard in class, take careful notes, and use as much time as she needed to try to decipher the words in her books. She graduated as one of the top students in her class and was accepted at Radcliffe College, the sister college of Harvard University.

Two years later, Helen decided to transfer to the University of California at Berkeley. She explained later, "At Radcliffe I was known as my father's daughter."[2] Helen hoped that in California she could establish an independent identity. At Berkeley she enjoyed acting in school plays, playing tennis, and hiking. When she graduated, she knew she was interested in pursuing a medical degree.

Her father suggested that Helen consider getting a degree at Harvard's School of Public Health. When she went to talk to the dean of admissions, however, she was told that "women will be permitted to study . . . but not admitted as candidates for degrees."

"Who'd be such a fool," Helen demanded, "to spend . . . years studying . . . and not get a degree?"

"No one, I hope," the dean replied.

"I will not be the first one to disappoint you," Helen said, walking out the door. "Good afternoon."[3]

At this time, there were only about 7,000 female physicians in the entire United States—only 6 percent of all doctors.[4] Helen was determined to join this small group.

She decided to take an anatomy course at Boston University. During this class, her teacher shoved the heart of an ox into her hands and said, "Here. It wouldn't hurt you to become interested in a major organ of the body."[5] Little did he know that one day his student would become one of the leading heart specialists in the country.

Helen studied the heart, dissected it, and examined the tissues and performed experiments upon them. "Finally," she recalled, "it got all mauled up and I thought it was the only beef heart I was ever going to have."[6] But her professor was impressed by her preliminary work and gave her another fresh heart to continue working on.

This time Helen tried to set up an experiment that would make small strips of heart muscle contract on their own. Researchers had been able to do this with strips of muscles from cold-blooded animals, but never with muscles from a mammal, like an ox. After much experimentation and trial and error, Helen lowered a scrap of muscle into a specially prepared solution and watched the muscle contract. The results of her experiments were published in a leading medical journal.

Helen's anatomy professor realized that she was a student with uncommon potential and recommended that she apply to the medical program at Johns Hopkins University. Not only was it one of the nation's leading medical schools, but unlike some other institutions, it also admitted women. This was because in 1889 a group of women promised to offer Johns Hopkins money for their medical school on the condition that women be admitted on the same terms as men. The financially strapped Johns Hopkins surrendered to the women's terms.

Helen transferred to Johns Hopkins and after four years of intensive study received her M.D. in 1927. Immediately upon graduating, Helen as well as most of the other women graduates, applied for an internship at the same institution. Only one woman would receive this position, and Helen was disappointed to learn that she had narrowly lost. Instead, she went to work with the university's heart clinic, and in 1930 joined the brand-new pediatric cardiology department. This was a new field of medicine, and often Helen felt frustrated that there were not more-effective ways of treating the children's various heart problems.

At this time, Helen had also noticed that she was having trouble hearing. Her beloved classical music no longer sounded as rich as it did before. Sometimes she could barely hear the quieter parts of a symphony and would double-check to make sure her radio was still turned on.

During the next year, her hearing further deteriorated for reasons doctors could never determine. Helen was terribly worried. One of her most important tools to examine patients was her stethoscope, but she could no longer hear the children's heartbeats. She knew she had to find a way to compensate for this loss. Helen discovered that by pressing her hands firmly, but not too firmly, on the child's chest, she could feel the heart contracting. She would later startle her colleagues by being able to detect the slightest heart murmurs with her hands, which they had been unable to pick up with their stethoscopes.

Helen's other concern was to find a way to communicate with her patients and their families. She began wearing a hearing aid and learning to lip-read. Even so, there were times when she could not understand what people were saying and would ask them to write down their thoughts. In this way, she was able to continue her work and care for her patients.

Helen Taussig had a gentleness that instantly calmed frightened children. She would always explain what she was doing during her exams. One of her most useful pieces of equipment often seemed frightening to children, but she promised them that it would not hurt. It was called a fluoroscope and worked rather like an X-ray machine, but instead of giving a doctor pictures of bones, it would illuminate the child's heart.

Helen would take her patient into a dark room, then turn on the fluoroscope and be able to see the heart beating and the nearby blood vessels. By asking the child to move, she could see the heart from various angles. Often she would have to work very hard to discover the elusive defects in a child's heart. Sometimes her patients would be too sick to be helped. When a child died, Dr. Taussig would always go to the autopsy and carefully study the heart to gain valuable information.

The human heart is a powerful muscle in charge of pumping blood all over the body. It is responsible for pumping blood to the lungs, where the blood can pick up oxygen, and then pumping the oxygenated blood to the rest of the body. This oxygenated blood is bright red and gives the skin of light-skinned people its pinkish color. After blood has given up its oxygen, it turns bluish. This bluish blood returns to the heart and then is pumped back to the lungs, where it can once again pick up oxygen and continue the cycle.

In the late 1930s Dr. Taussig was seeing a number of young children with heart problems who had a bluish tinge to their skin, lips, and fingernails. This was because their blood did not have enough oxygen in it, a condition doctors called "cyanotic," which is derived from the Greek word *kyanosis*, which means "dark blue." The less oxygen in the child's blood, the bluer the child. Normal activities such as walking down a hallway were extraordinarily difficult for some of these children. They would take a few steps, then fall to the floor gasping for breath. Sometimes they would faint or even enter a coma from a lack of oxygen. It was as if they were suffocating even while they were breathing.

No one had been able to pinpoint exactly why these cyanotic children did not have enough oxygen in their blood. Most doctors assumed that there was some defect in their hearts.

Dr. Taussig used her fluoroscope and autopsies to study minute details of cyanotic children's hearts. Gradually she determined that many of the children had problems associated with their pulmonary arteries. This artery is the main blood vessel connecting the heart and the lungs. In some cyanotic children, the pulmonary artery was too small to allow adequate blood to flow from the heart to the lungs.

To help these children, Helen reasoned, she needed to find a way for more blood to get to the lungs. She began focusing on a vessel called the ductus arteriosus. This is a vessel that normally exists only in fetuses. Fetuses get their oxygen from their mothers through the placenta. Therefore, blood does not flow to the lungs of the fetus to get oxygenated. The ductus arteriosus connects the pulmonary artery with the aorta, the main vessel that allows blood to go to the rest of the body. When a baby is born and takes its first few breaths, blood is pumped to the lungs and the ductus arteriosus shuts off and withers away. If this vessel doesn't shut off, too much blood is sent to the lungs, damaging the tissue.

But, Dr. Taussig thought, sending more blood to the lungs of cyanotic children would not be a problem; it was just what their oxygen-starved bodies needed. She reasoned that if there was a way to keep the ductus arteriosis open in cyanotic children or to re-create such a vessel through an operation, more blood would be able to flow to their lungs and therefore more blood could be oxygenated.

In 1939 she learned about a doctor named Robert Gross who had received great acclaim for developing an operation to close the ductus on otherwise healthy children. If he could tie it off, Dr. Taussig thought, perhaps he could find a way to open the ductus or create a new one in a blue baby. She rushed to Boston to meet with Dr. Gross. By developing the operation, he had done "a very remarkable thing . . ." she later said. "And everybody was congratulating him."[7] However, he was not certain that opening the ductus would produce successful results.

Frustrated but not beaten, Dr. Taussig remained convinced that if a ductus could be kept open or reconstructed, it would save the lives of her patients. She had not been trained in surgery, so she did not have the technical knowledge to do the operation herself. She would need to wait to find a surgeon willing to take a chance.

That man would arrive at Johns Hopkins in 1941. His name was Dr. Alfred Blalock. He was a famous surgeon who had successfully performed Dr. Gross's difficult operation to close a ductus three times in the past. Dr. Taussig took him aside and said, "I stand in awe and admiration of your surgical skill, but the really great day will come when you build a ductus for a cyanotic child, not when you tie off a ductus for a child who has a little too much blood going to his lungs."[8]

Dr. Blalock was ready to take on the challenge. He set up a laboratory and put the day-to-day research under the direction of a talented African-American scientist, Vivien Thomas. Thomas had been forced to quit his medical education for financial reasons but had begun working as a surgical researcher. Later he would be given an honorary doctorate and would become an instructor in surgery.

After much trial and error, Thomas managed to successfully create an artificial ductus in a dog named Anna. After recreating this surgery on almost two hundred other dogs,

Thomas, Dr. Blalock, and Dr. Taussig felt there was a reasonable chance it would work on a human child.

The first child was Eileen Saxon. At fifteen months, she weighed only nine and a half pounds (little more than most babies weigh at birth). When Dr. Taussig examined her, she knew that Eileen was very sick. Even in an oxygen tent, "she breathed fast and deep and then suddenly went limp and lost consciousness. After resting for a period of time, she spontaneously came to again . . . until another spell occurred."[9]

On November 29, 1944, Dr. Taussig and Vivien Thomas watched Dr. Blalock open Eileen's tiny chest cavity and with great skill build a new ductus that was as small as a matchstick. Eileen lived for another six months, but then died during another operation.

In 1945 Dr. Blalock performed similar operations on two more children. The second of these was, as Dr. Taussig recalled, "on a small, utterly miserable, six-year-old boy who . . . was no longer able to walk."[10] After Dr. Blalock created a ductus, however, the anesthesiologist said suddenly, "The boy's a lovely color now!" Walking around to the head of the table, Dr. Taussig saw his healthy, pink lips. The child went on to lead a healthy, happy, and active life.

As soon as news of the miraculous operation spread through the press, Dr. Taussig was inundated with new patients. In the next six years, she saw over three thousand cyanotic children and Dr. Blalock performed over a thousand surgeries. At first some doctors worried that the cyanotic children might have suffered brain damage as a result of their prolonged lack of oxygen, but in studies Dr. Taussig compiled years later, it was clear that a very high percent became intelligent and accomplished adults.

The success of these operations encouraged surgeons to dare to perform other types of surgery on the heart—which before had seemed almost unimaginable to operate on. "The result," one of their colleagues said, "is much of present-day cardiac surgery."[11]

Despite her tremendous contribution to cardiac medicine, Dr. Taussig was initially overlooked, largely because she was a woman. While Dr. Blalock was elected to the prestigious National Academy of Sciences, she was not. In 1941 he was promoted to full professor, but Dr. Taussig was not allowed to receive a similar position. In fact, it was not until 1946 that she would be promoted to the lesser rank of associate professor and not until 1959 that she would become a full professor. She said, "Over the years I've gotten recognition for what I did, but I didn't at the time. It hurt for a while."[12]

Numerous young doctors sought the opportunity to work with and learn from Dr. Taussig. Training new doctors became one of the great joys of her career. She also enjoyed entertaining friends and colleagues at her lovely home, and it was at such a dinner that she first learned from a friend about a terrible birth defect affecting children in Germany.

"He began to tell me about all the limbless babies being born . . . ," Dr. Taussig recalled. "He mentioned that some investigators had implicated a drug."[13] At this time, there was still very little research about the effects of drugs on unborn children. But Dr. Taussig recognized a potential tragedy in the making. She immediately applied for and received a grant to go to Europe to learn what she could.

Traveling to clinics in Great Britain and Germany, she examined numerous children with a horrible birth defect, called "phocomelia," or "seal limb." Instead of arms, they had small flipperlike appendages at their shoulders, as well as deformed or missing legs. In the early 1950s only about fifteen cases of "seal limb" had been reported, but in 1959 alone there were twelve cases, and in 1961 twenty-six children were born with this deformity.

The cause seemed to be a sleeping pill called thalidomide. Doctors had previously thought thalidomide had no side effects, but gradually researchers were coming to realize that some women who had taken these pills during pregnancy had given birth to seal-limb children.

In the United States thalidomide was being studied by the Food and Drug Administration (FDA). Dr. Frances Kelsey, an FDA physician, had decided to withhold permission to market the drug until she learned more about it. When Dr. Taussig returned home with data about the seal-limb babies, Dr. Kelsey resolved not to allow the drug to be marketed in America.

Dr. Taussig knew there was still a chance, however, that people might gain access to thalidomide by purchasing it overseas. Also, drug companies sometimes gave physicians trial drugs to hand out to patients before they were approved by the FDA. Dr. Taussig wanted to ensure that no doctors administered trial batches of thalidomide. She began a campaign to warn the public about its awful side effects. She published articles in important scientific publications that were then picked up by newspapers all across the country. Dr. Taussig did not stop there. She urged Congress to strengthen the Food and Drug Act to protect consumers from other new experimental drugs. In 1963 Congress passed a law requiring more-thorough testing before drugs could be sold.

That same year, Helen Taussig retired from Johns Hopkins, although she continued to travel across the country advocating children's health-care needs. In 1964 President Lyndon B. Johnson awarded her the Medal of Freedom, the highest honor that can be bestowed on an American citizen. The next year she became the first woman ever to be elected president of the American Heart Association. For many years after, Helen Taussig continued to publish important articles in various medical journals.

On May 20, 1986, she was killed in an automobile accident. She had summed up her career in a letter she wrote in 1976 when she said, "I personally feel, and think I have proven, that if you can make your contribution and do significant work, the world will respect you, men and women alike."[14]

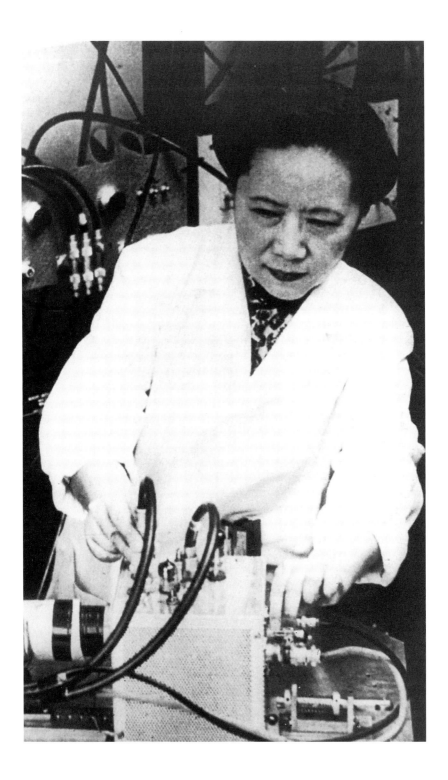

NINE

CHIEN-SHIUNG WU

Nuclear physicist Chien-Shiung (pronounced Chen Shung) Wu once remarked that she was probably one of the first scientists ever to win world acclaim "not for establishing a law, but for overthrowing it."[1] She devised a tremendously complicated and difficult experiment that definitively proved that one of the long-held laws of physics was not always correct. From the start, she knew there was very little chance of success—she estimated that the odds against her were one million to one. But Chien-Shiung was willing to take a chance and her perseverance paid off. As the New York Times reported, "This small modest woman was powerful enough to do what armies can never accomplish: She helped destroy a law of nature. And laws of nature, by their very definition, should be constant, continuous, immutable, indestructible."[2]

Chien-Shiung Wu was born on May 29, 1912. She grew up with her two brothers in a town called Liu Ho, about thirty miles from Shanghai, China. "I had a fortunate and happy childhood," Chien-Shiung said.[3] She was lucky to have a father who believed that society should treat women and men as intellectual equals. At that time this was a radical philosophy. Chinese women were expected to be subservient to men and were not given the same educational opportunities.

To try to help change this, Chien-Shiung's father decided to start the first girls' school in their region. When Chien-Shiung was young, the school had only the first four grades. After she graduated, she left her close-knit family to continue her education at Soochow, a prestigious girls' boarding school.

There, she had to choose between the teachers' training program and the college preparatory school. Chien-Shiung chose the former because it was free and guaranteed her a job after graduation. She soon realized that her friends in the academic school were learning a great deal more about science. After her friends finished studying, she would borrow their textbooks. In this way, she began teaching herself physics and chemistry.

During this time, China was experiencing a period of great unrest. Japan was preparing to invade it, and in response a student nationalist movement arose in support of the president, Chiang Kai-shek, and his efforts to resist a takeover. Chien-Shiung Wu's friends convinced her to become their leader, and she began representing the students at marches and protests.

In 1930 she graduated from Soochow with the highest grades in the school and won admittance to the prestigious National Central University in Nanjing. She was interested in physics, but was worried that without having taken classes in this subject, she would not know enough to compete successfully. She thought it might be safer to study education.

When she told her father of this decision, he shook his head and said that she had ample time to catch up. "Later that day," Chien-Shiung recalled, "he came home with one textbook on high algebra and a textbook each on physics and chemistry as well. I was elated to receive these books all at once. I studied them that summer at home."[4]

In September 1930 she enrolled in the physics program and quickly became one of the best students. In fact, one afternoon a number of the school's professors got together in the faculty lounge and began discussing their most outstanding student. They were surprised to discover that they had all been talking about the same young woman—Chien-Shiung Wu.

Chien-Shiung realized that China offered no graduate-level courses in physics and that she would have to leave if she wanted to pursue a Ph.D. She picked the University of California at Berkeley for her graduate work. "That," she said, "was the golden age for the physics department at Berkeley. Berkeley was at the top of the world."[5] Despite the tough competition, Chien-Shiung found she had more trouble adapting to the odd American cafeteria food than to her academic workload. Once again she was at the top of her class. More exciting, she had learned about the relatively new subject of nuclear physics.

Her excitement was tempered, however, by the troubling course of world events. One morning, at the end of her first year at Berkeley, she was shocked to read the newspaper headline "Japan Invades China."[6] In the next few days, she read horrifying reports of Japanese troops raping and murdering an estimated 42,000 civilians. Chien-Shiung prayed that her family was all right.

The physics department rallied around its top student. Her professors knew she had been cut off from her family's financial support and promised to help her receive financial aid so that she could continue her studies. Chien-Shiung felt bound to repay their confidence by doing her best and would often stay in the lab late into the night, long after everyone else had left. She said, "I have always felt that in physics and probably in other endeavors, too, you have total commitment. It is not just a job. It is a way of life."[7]

Her hard work paid off and in 1940 she received her Ph.D. with top honors. She remained at Berkeley, taking a job as a research assistant and gradually establishing a reputation as a young and talented expert on nuclear fission. Despite her renown, Berkeley refused to promote her. For one thing, she was a woman. At the time, the twenty top research universities did not have a single woman on their physics faculties. If they had a choice between a male candidate and a female one, they picked the male, whether or not he was better qualified. Also, the United States had begun to fight against the Japanese in World War II and anyone who was of Asian descent was regarded with suspicion—including the Chinese, even though they had been the primary victims of Japanese aggression and had been at war with Japan for five years.

Frustrated by this discrimination, Chien-Shiung remembered that a friend had offered her a teaching job if she ever wanted it at Smith College in Northampton, Massachusetts. In 1942 she packed her things and moved to the East Coast. Earlier that same year, she had married Luke Yuan, a former Berkeley classmate and fellow physicist. Luke took a job at a lab in New Jersey, and they visited each other on the weekends.

Although Chien-Shiung enjoyed her job, she regretted that the college did not have adequate research facilities. She decided to apply for teaching jobs at other, better-equipped universities and won appointments to all of them. This, she knew, had less to do with her ability than with the fact that many male physicists had been recruited by the government to work on war weapons. As a result, universities were in desperate need of physics teachers. In fact, many of them that offered Chien-Shiung a job refused to admit female students to their physics programs.

Twenty-seven year old Chien-Shiung decided to accept Princeton's offer since it had a first-class research lab. A few months later, however, she was asked to report for an interview at the Division of War Research at Columbia University in New York City. For hours she was quizzed about her research by two physicists who offered no information about their department's secret war projects. Finally at the end, after they had decided to hire her, one of the men asked, "Now Miss Wu, do you know anything about what we're doing here?"

"I'm sorry," she smiled, "but if you wanted me not to know what you're doing, you should have cleaned the blackboards."[8]

Their secret work was known as the Manhattan Project, and it resulted in the development of the atomic bomb. Chien-Shiung realized that by working with them she would be able to help the war effort against the Japanese, something she was very eager to do. Her research focused mainly on developing instruments to detect radiation. After the war, she was one of the few Manhattan Project scientists offered a job at Columbia University as a research associate.

In 1947 she gave birth to a son, Vincent. Soon after, she and Luke applied to become U.S. citizens, and in 1954 they were awarded citizenship.

Throughout the late 1940s and early 1950s, Chien-Shiung was performing exciting research on beta decay. Beta decay occurs when the nucleus of a large radioactive atom spontaneously ejects a superfast electron and a neutrino (an uncharged elementary particle with zero mass), and in this natural process turns into another element. Normally, electrons remain outside of an atom and do not reside in the nucleus. In beta decay, however, a neutron inside the nucleus breaks into a neutrino, a proton, and an electron. In this state, the nucleus has excessive energy. To rid it of the energy, the neutrino and electron burst out of the nucleus. The proton is left behind in the new and relatively more stable nucleus.

In 1933 Italian physicist Enrico Fermi had proposed that the electrons bursting out of the nucleus would travel at extraordinarily high speeds. But all scientific studies found only slow-moving electrons after beta decay.

Studying these experiments, Chien-Shiung realized that the researchers had used materials of uneven thickness. She reasoned that the electrons that had been shot out from beta decay slowed down as they hit the uneven sections and lost speed. This was why they seemed to move so slowly.

Chien-Shiung developed a new experiment using a material that was uniformly thin to study beta decay. She found that the electrons did indeed move at tremendous speeds as Fermi had predicted. Her work was meticulous, her results precise. In this and other experiments, she quickly established a reputation for being a demanding and perfectionistic researcher. Her results, everyone knew, could be trusted.

One colleague said, "She always chose to do the significant and important experiments—no matter how difficult they were. And they were very difficult to do."[9]

Her reputation led two young Chinese-American researchers named Tsung Dao Lee and Chen Ning Yang to ask her for help. They wanted to devise an experiment that would explain what was known by nuclear physicists as the "tau-theta puzzle."

With the advent of new atom-smashing devices in the 1950s, scientists had found that when certain atomic nuclei were broken, short-lived particles called K-mesons flew out. The problem was that the actions of two of these particles, known as tau and theta, did not obey what was called the law of parity.

The law of parity was a long-held law of nature that stated that all nuclear objects and their mirror images behave the same way, but with the left hand and right hand reversed. To understand this, imagine that someone is standing with a corkscrew in one hand and a corked bottle in the other. By revolving the corkscrew in a clockwise motion, the cork comes out. If this person were looking at herself in a mirror, it would appear that the corkscrew was turning counterclockwise, and yet the cork still comes out. The law of parity says that nature does not care whether one looks at an experiment in real life or in a mirror. Whether you look directly at the person turning the corkscrew or look at the person's image in the mirror, the result is the same—the cork comes out.

Lee and Yang and a few other scientists had noticed that with K-mesons, the law of parity did not seem to hold. These particles sometimes seemed to favor one direction over another. (In effect, they might seem to prefer turning counterclockwise, rather than clockwise.)

It is not important for us to understand exactly why, but according to the law of parity, when the K-mesons tau and theta broke down, they should have done so in the same way, but they did not. Instead, the tau mesons broke down into three particles, and the theta mesons broke down into two particles.

Most physicists thought that there must be some sort of experimental error that was causing these K-mesons to disobey the law of parity. Lee and Yang, however, thought that maybe the law of parity was not valid in all instances. Perhaps it held only for things outside of atomic nuclei, but inside the nuclei other factors could be at work. They wrote up their queries in a paper in 1956.

It was a radical notion. "This law," one writer noted, "had been built into all physical theories for three decades. So universally had it been accepted it was almost as unthinkable for a scientist to cast doubt on the principle of parity as on the law of gravitation."[10]

To find a way to prove that the law of parity was not valid

inside an atomic nucleus would require tremendously difficult and arduous experiments. No one wanted to take on this challenge. But Lee and Yang decided to turn to Chien-Shiung Wu for assistance. Even they doubted that she would find a way to demonstrate that the law of parity did not hold in the nuclei. But the more Chien-Shiung thought about this challenge, the more exciting it seemed.

Although she was scheduled to go on a romantic cruise with her husband, she postponed the trip to begin devising an experiment. She knew that her own self-doubts could easily get in the way and tried to force them to the back of her mind.

"Many things worried me," Chien-Shiung later said. "Very often in doing these experiments, something goes wrong. Most physicists thought we would find nothing exciting. The odds were one million to one in their favor that the law of parity . . . was conserved. In fact, many famous physicists bet on it."[11]

Although the experiment she devised was relatively simple conceptually, it was very difficult to set up. Chien-Shiung wanted to study the nuclei in a radioactive form of cobalt called cobalt-60. Her plan was to put the cobalt into a magnetic field many times greater than that of the earth's magnetic field. This would force the nuclei to line up like little magnets in a straight row. The magnetic field would not affect the radiation of the cobalt, so it would continue to disintegrate. As it did, it would shoot out electrons. Dr. Wu hoped to be able to watch where the electrons went. If they shot out equally in opposite directions, the law of parity would hold in the nucleus. If they favored one direction over the other, it would not.

The problem, however, was that at room temperature, heat energy made the nuclei move around so much, it was impossible to tell which direction their electrons were shooting with any accuracy. To slow down their motion, she would have to cool the cobalt-60 to near absolute zero (-459.67 degrees Fahrenheit), the temperature at which all atomic motion due to heat is stopped.

At this time, there was only one research facility in the United States that had the equipment that could cool material to near absolute zero—the National Bureau of Standards in Washington, D.C. Wu solicited its help, and for the next six months she averaged four hours of sleep a night, working in Washington and then returning to Columbia to teach her classes. "It was," she said, "like a nightmare I wouldn't want to go through again."[12]

One reason the experiment took so long was that she was forced to construct much of the equipment herself. For example, she had to find a way to make a tiny box for the cobalt during the freezing process. It had to be made out of cerium magnesium nitrate crystals (CMN). Halfway through the project, Wu and her researchers realized that no one knew how to make CMN. But then, on a dusty back shelf they found a long-forgotten, yellowed German text from the nineteenth century that described how to make CMN. They used glue to try to construct the crystals into a box shape, but the box fell apart near absolute zero. They tried using soap to stick the crystals together. First they tried one brand of dish detergent, which worked well. But another brand was even better. Finally it turned out that common nylon string worked the best.

When the experiment was finally ready, they froze the cobalt-60 and examined the motion of the electrons. A majority of the electrons were ejected in one direction—the direction opposite the one in which the nucleus was spinning. Chien-Shiung did the experiment a few more times with different conditions, and they all showed the same thing. She could hardly believe it—she'd proven that the law of parity was sometimes violated!

"After the discovery," she said, "I couldn't sleep for about two weeks. Why should the Lord want to tell this secret through me?"[13]

This discovery shocked the scientific world and captured the imagination of the public at large. Wu was featured in *Time* and *Newsweek* and given numerous honorary doctorates, including the first honorary doctorate of science that Princeton University had ever bestowed upon a woman. At the ceremony, Princeton's president announced that Dr. Wu had "richly earned the right to be called the world's foremost female experimental physicist."[14]

She also became the first woman to win the Comstock Award from the National Academy of Sciences, an honor that is given only once every five years. One award, however, that she did not receive was the Nobel Prize. Lee and Yang were given this honor ten months after Wu's experiment was completed, and she, as well as many other physicists, were disappointed that she had not been included in this recognition.

Her life, however, had been forever changed by her experiment. In recognition for her outstanding work, Columbia University made her a full professor. Many theoretical scientists also began begging Dr. Wu to devise experiments to prove their hypotheses. One particularly persistent researcher, Murray Gell-Mann, wanted her to test his theory that energy called "vector current" is conserved during the disintegration of nuclear particles. Experiments designed by top researchers at prestigious laboratories all over the world had failed to confirm the theory.

"How long did Yang and Lee pursue you to follow up their work?" he asked,[15] planning to pursue her even longer until she agreed.

Finally Chien-Shiung told him she would devise a way to test his theory. The experiment she set up succeeded in proving a law this time, rather than toppling it. She conclusively showed that vector current is conserved. It was not as startling as her earlier experiment, but still fundamentally important.

In her later career, Wu began trying to use her skill and intellect to better understand a disease called sickle-cell anemia, which affects mainly African Americans. Although Dr. Wu did not succeed, she said that her work showed that "even the most sophisticated and remote basic nuclear physics research has implications beneficial to human welfare."[16]

In 1976 President Gerald Ford presented her with the country's highest science award, the National Medal of Science. In 1981 Wu retired from Columbia University and began traveling all over the world, lecturing and encouraging women to pursue careers in science.

"Science is not static, but ever-growing and dynamic . . . ," she once said. "It is the courage to doubt what has long been established, the incessant search for its verification and proof that pushed the wheel of science forward."[17]

TEN

ROSALYN YALOW

The Nobel Prize was established by a Swedish man named Alfred Nobel. He had become one of the richest men in the world after discovering dynamite. In his handwritten will, he designated that his millions be used to fund an award that would honor those individuals whose achievements or discoveries had done the most to help humankind in the previous year. Generally considered the most prestigious award in the world, the Nobel is given in six fields: physics, chemistry, medicine or physiology, literature, peace, and economics. The first Nobel Prize was awarded in 1901.

In 1977 the Nobel Prize in Medicine was awarded to Rosalyn Yalow. She was only the sixth woman ever to win a Nobel and the first woman recipient who had been born and trained in the United States. At the awards banquet, she was further honored by being asked to give the main speech.

The king of Sweden, the other laureates, and numerous assembled guests and dignitaries waited while a university student walked down the long table to escort Dr. Yalow to the podium. He had assumed that Dr. Yalow was a man, and so he stopped behind the chair of Rosalyn Yalow's husband and waited for the man to rise and join him. But across the table, a dark-haired woman in a shimmering sequined vest stood and walked to the front of the room.

In her speech that evening, Rosalyn Yalow set forth a challenge to young women to use their intelligence and skills to benefit all people: "We must believe in ourselves," she said. "Or no one else will believe in us; we must match our aspirations with the competence, courage, and determination to succeed, and we must feel a personal responsibility to ease the path for those who come afterward."[1]

Rosalyn Sussman was born on July 19, 1921, in the South Bronx section of New York City. Both of her parents were first-generation American Jews who had not been educated beyond elementary school. They were determined that Rosalyn and her older brother, Alexander, would one day go to college.

Rosalyn's father had a small paper and twine business, and her mother sewed piecework for an uncle's neckwear company. During the Depression the family had no money to spare. When Rosalyn needed braces for her teeth, she helped her mother sew at night to earn enough money to pay the orthodontist. "If you wanted something," she recalled, "you worked for it. It didn't keep me from doing my homework."[2]

Rosalyn was an excellent student, especially in math, and skipped a number of grades. At fifteen, she graduated from high school and went to New York's Hunter College. This school provided a tuition-free education to any young woman with sufficiently high grades. At Hunter, Rosalyn took her first physics course and immediately fell in love with the subject. She was further inspired by reading the biography of Madame Curie, the remarkable French woman scientist who discovered radioactivity.

Rosalyn was convinced she wanted to become a physicist, despite the fact that Hunter did not offer a degree program in this science. A classmate recalled that she was "very single-minded. She knew—*absolutely knew*—she was going to become a physicist."[3] Rosalyn arranged to take a night course in physics at the City College of New York, and the science department at Hunter helped establish a new physics degree program especially for her. Rosalyn graduated with top honors—magna cum laude—and was elected to the honor society Phi Beta Kappa. She looked forward to continuing her study of physics in graduate school.

Rosalyn quickly realized, however, that to do so she would have to overcome sexual discrimination and anti-Semitism. It was widely assumed that since males were considered the primary breadwinners in most families, they should have first shot at graduate studies. There were very few openings for equally or even more qualified women. When Rosalyn applied to one university's physics program, the school wrote back to her professor, "She's a Jew and a woman and we can never get her a job afterward."[4]

Rosalyn decided that her only hope was to try get into a program through the back door. On the advice of one of her professors, she agreed to take a job as a secretary at Columbia University. As an employee, she would be allowed to take courses at the college. Rosalyn hoped that she would be able to impress her professors with her intelligence and eventually win admittance.

During the summer of 1940, she took a class in shorthand to prepare herself for her secretarial duties. Within six weeks, however, the most prestigious school she had applied to, the University of Illinois, offered her a spot in its physics program. Rosalyn tore up her stenographer's notebooks and started to pack immediately.

She knew she had won the spot because World War II had caused a significant drop in male enrollments in university graduate programs. Many young men were fighting overseas, and their absence left opportunities open to women who, except for the war, would have been turned aside in favor of men. When Rosalyn entered the University of Illinois in 1941, she was the first woman since 1917 enrolled in the physics department and the only woman among four hundred male students. She knew that fate had given her such an opportunity, and she was determined to prove to everyone that a woman could hold her own and even shine in this predominantly male field.

Almost immediately she felt she was not adequately prepared to compete with men from top physics programs around the country. To catch up, Rosalyn sat in on undergraduate physics classes and spent long hours studying textbooks. Her hard work paid off. She received A's in her courses and an A- in her lab work. The chairman of the department said that the A- just went to prove what he had believed all along, that women were not outstanding at lab work!

Many years later, Rosalyn said, "The trouble with discrimination is that the victims believe it . . . . [But] I never thought there was anything the matter with me. I just felt sorry for the discriminators. There was never a time when I didn't do what I wanted."[5]

Rosalyn wanted a husband and a family. She said, "By the time I was 8, my idea of what my grown-up life would be was that I'd be a working scientist. . . . I also knew that I'd be married and have children."[6]

In her first days at Illinois, she met Aaron Yalow, a fellow physics major and the son of a rabbi. Soon they began dating seriously. During this time, Rosalyn continued to pursue her studies with passion and dedication, proving to herself and others that it was possible to balance a relationship and work.

Rosalyn's specialized field of study was nuclear physics. At this time during World War II, many top American scientists were working to develop the atomic bomb. The year that

Rosalyn received her Ph.D., the bombs were dropped on Hiroshima and Nagasaki.

This was also the year that she and Aaron planned to be married. "My husband," Rosalyn recalled, "took his comprehensive [final oral exams] about a week before we were married—the head of the department had it in for me, and if Aaron were going to marry me, it spilled over to him, too. So he asked Aaron a question, and made Aaron prove it 12 different ways."[7]

When it was time for Rosalyn to take her comprehensive exam, she was determined not to let this man upset her. When he told her that one of her answers was incorrect, she informed him that this was the way two other members of her examining committee had taught it to her, and if he had a quarrel with it, he better bring it up with them. Furious, the chairman stormed out of the room. Rosalyn easily passed what turned out to be one of the shortest exams ever and became only the second woman ever to receive a physics degree from the University of Illinois.

After their wedding in 1943, the Yalows moved back to New York City, and their first house was in a converted garage. Rosalyn recalled it "was sort of a gathering place. We used to leave a window open so people could come and go."[8]

Aaron also introduced his wife to a respected medical physicist named Edith Quimby. Dr. Quimby was studying medical uses of radioactivity. Rosalyn was fascinated by this subject and asked her if she could work in her lab. Rosalyn so impressed her employer that Dr. Quimby helped get her a position as a consultant at the Bronx Veterans Administration (VA) Hospital. At the age of twenty-six, Rosalyn was put in charge of the new radioisotope lab they had set up in a converted janitor's closet. Radioisotopes were used at the time as an inexpensive alternative to radium in the treatment of cancer. This had become possible after a nuclear plant began producing them quite cheaply.

An isotope is a name given to a group of atoms of a single chemical element that all have the same number of neutrons in their nuclei. A chemical element is a substance that can't be broken down into a simpler substance by ordinary chemical means or that contains only one type of atom. For example, hydrogen and oxygen are both chemical elements. Each element has a characteristic number of protons in the nuclei of its atoms, but the number of neutrons may vary from atom to atom. Each variation is known as an isotope. Some elements, such as sodium and cobalt, have only one stable isotope while others have more. Tin, for example, has ten isotopes.

Rosalyn's childhood hero, Marie Curie, had discovered that elements may also have radioactive isotopes. Radioactive isotopes are those with unstable atoms that decay or break down over time. As they decay, they emit penetrating radioactive rays. Rosalyn wanted to find medical uses for radioisotopes. She became part of a small group of scientists interested in the beneficial uses of radioactivity, which was the basis of the new and exciting field of nuclear medicine.

For many people, nuclear reactors and radioactivity are frightening concepts. The threat of nuclear war is a real possibility, and nuclear weapons could bring utter destruction. But in the late 1940s when Rosalyn Yalow was setting up her laboratory, nuclear power was seen as primarily a great and powerful tool. Even now, she is adamant about her belief that nuclear science is about saving life rather than ending it. She is an outspoken critic of opponents to all forms of nuclear power.

"There is a pervasive fear of radiation," she has said, "that is not borne out by the facts. A lot of money has been spent investigating low-level radiation."[9] She points out that low-level radiation has always been with us. She likes to cite the discovery that people in Denver are twice as strongly affected by radiation from cosmic rays and radioactive rocks as people living in New York City. But those in New York are twice as likely to have cancer as those in Denver. The point, she believes, is that in our fear of nuclear war, we have needlessly attacked the entire field of nuclear science, even though certain branches of nuclear science can save lives.

When Rosalyn began her work in the VA hospital lab, she realized that much of the equipment she would need for her research was not commercially available. Therefore, she set about building it herself. Within her first two years at the lab, Rosalyn published eight scientific papers on discoveries she had made about radioisotopes. She was also teaching courses at Hunter College and managing a kosher household. It is hard to imagine how she had time for all of this, but every day she woke up feeling invigorated by the research she was doing in her lab.

Some of her most intriguing work was investigating the possible uses of radioisotopes to further understand the chemical and biological processes of the human body. In order to do so, she knew she would need to spend more time in the lab, so in 1950 she resigned from the faculty at Hunter College. Her students were devastated. They loved having a young teacher who was doing such exciting, cutting-edge research.

Rosalyn also realized she would need the help and expertise of someone trained in internal medicine to assist her. The hospital's medical chief recommended that she try working with a young doctor named Solomon Berson. This was the start of a remarkably fruitful collaboration that would last until Berson's death in 1972.

Sol Berson was a "renaissance man," or someone who is versed in a variety of subjects. He was a master chess player and a talented violinist. He was also, Rosalyn said, "a bit of . . . [a] male chauvinist pig. . . . He expected women to walk two steps behind him."[10] In public, Rosalyn Yalow was willing to play second fiddle. For example, if they were asked to give a speech about their work, Sol Berson would be the one to step up to the microphone, but Rosalyn would have arranged for their plane tickets, typed up the speech, packed their lunches, and made their hotel arrangements.

"[Sol] was a leader in everything that he did," she said, "and it would have been very upsetting to him if I did not defer. And really there was nothing [for me] to lose."[11] Perhaps the reason Rosalyn could feel this way was that she knew that in the lab they were absolute equals.

They set up their desks facing each other so that they could bounce ideas off one another, see where their imaginations could take them. When an interesting idea struck them, they'd go rushing off to the lab, their white coats fluttering behind. Sometimes they worked nearly around the clock, leaving the lab in the middle of the night and coming back to their desks soon after dawn. During this time, Rosalyn also managed to continue to cook and clean her own house.

She also dreamed of one day becoming a mother, but first she wanted to make herself irreplaceable at the VA because the hospital had a rule that women could not work past their fifth month of pregnancy. When Rosalyn finally did decide to become pregnant, everyone ignored this rule, and she worked up until the day her son, Benjamin, was born. "They needed me," she said.[12]

She was back at work a week later, lugging Benjamin with her. Fortunately, he slept through most of the day while she and Sol were working. At night, Rosalyn often would let Aaron sleep while she would stay up and take care of the baby. Many nights she'd sleep for only an hour or two. When her pediatrician told her he disapproved of her decision to continue working, she said with customary feistiness, "Doctor, that's your problem," and she promptly switched to a new pediatrician.[13]

Two years after Ben was born, she gave birth to a daughter, Elanna. The Yalows decided to hire someone to help take care of the children during the day and to clean the house.

Every noon, however, Rosalyn would come home from work to eat lunch with the children. Often she would take them to the lab with her so they could play with the animals. She was also the one neighborhood mother who could be counted on to chaperone everyone to the zoo and museums. Rosalyn had always been convinced she could be a superwife, a supermom, and a superscientist.

The technique for which she would eventually win the Nobel Prize "came into being almost by accident," Rosalyn said. "It was an offshoot of another investigation."[14] She and Sol had been using radioactive iodine to tag insulin, which is made in the pancreas. Our bodies use insulin to process sugar for energy. Adults with the disease diabetes have unusually high levels of sugar in their blood. It was assumed that this was because diabetics did not produce enough insulin. To help them process sugar, doctors injected diabetics with insulin from cattle or sheep.

One of Sol and Rosalyn's colleagues suggested that there might be an enzyme in diabetics that attacked their insulin, and they set out to learn if this was true. They injected themselves as well as some volunteers, including people with diabetes, with radioactively tagged insulin. If there was an insulin-killing enzyme in the diabetics, there would soon be few traces of the radioactive insulin in their bodies. But the opposite turned out to be true. The insulin remained in the diabetics longer than in anyone else. Why?

Dr. Yalow and Dr. Berson began pondering this surprising result, bouncing ideas off each other until finally they decided that the diabetics might have antibodies that were immobilizing the insulin. Our bodies produce antibodies to fight off foreign agents, such as germs. Rosalyn and Sol reasoned that diabetics who had been receiving regular injections of foreign insulin might have built up antibodies to it. This in turn might be keeping the insulin from being absorbed into their bodies.

From the insulin experiment, they developed a way to study the very small concentrations of insulin that are in human blood. They used radioactive animal insulin, insulin antibodies (obtained from guinea pigs), and a subject's blood containing its own insulin. This process became known as radioimmunoassay (RIA).

Berson and Yalow came to realize that by making some simple substitutions in the general formula, the RIA process could be used to measure not only insulin but also virtually any other substance in the human body! In fact, it was so precise that it would be able to detect the presence of a sugar cube in Lake Erie.

Today there are between fifty and sixty different RIA kits on the market that hospitals, labs, and individuals use for diagnosis and management of various conditions, including diabetes, thyroid disease, growth disorders, reproductive failures, and cancers. They are estimated to have a $30-million-a-year market, though none of these proceeds go to the inventors. "We did not patent the radioimmunoassay," Dr. Yalow said. "Scientists don't always think of things as being patentable. We made a scientific discovery. Once it was published, it was open to the world."[15]

RIA's have also been used by the police to test for drugs and other substances in blood. And one pharmaceutical company has produced an RIA kit that corporations use to test employees for drug use.

At first, the remarkable impact of RIA was not immediately known. For five years, Drs. Yalow and Berson worked to publicize their discovery. By 1955 RIA was being widely used by doctors and scientists all over the world. When, in 1972, Sol Berson died of a heart attack, Rosalyn was devastated. A long and fruitful partnership was at an end. She named her laboratory at the VA after him and kept a photo of her partner on her desk.

Many assumed that with Sol's death, Rosalyn's chances

for winning the Nobel Prize were dashed. No scientist had ever won the award after his or her partner had passed away. Since only five women had ever won the prize before, it seemed her chances were slim.

But early on the morning of October 13, 1977, when Rosalyn was already working at her desk, she got the call from Stockholm. "For the first hour," she said, "I had no reaction—I was absolutely stunned."[16]

Since that time, Rosalyn Yalow has continued to work at the Bronx VA hospital on various applications for RIA and on promoting the safe use of nuclear energy.

SOURCE NOTES

ONE: MILDRED DRESSELHAUS

1. Sharon Bertsch McGrayne, *Nobel Prize Women in Science: Their Lives, Struggles, and Momentous Discoveries* (Secaucus, N.J.: Carol Publishing Group, 1993), 381.

2. Ibid., 342.

3. Sam Merrill, "Women in Engineering," *Cosmopolitan*, April 1976, 164.

4. Ibid., 164.

5. Ibid., 166.

6. Mildred S. Dresselhaus, "Perspectives on the Presidency of the American Physical Society," *Physics Today*, July 1985, 38–39.

7. Merrill, "Women in Engineering," 164.

8. Iris Noble, *Contemporary Women Scientists of America* (New York: Messner, 1979), 149.

9. Mildred S. Dresselhaus, "Women Graduate Students," *Physics Today*, June 1986, 74.

10. Ibid., 74.

11. Merrill, "Women in Engineering," 164.

12. Dresselhaus, "Perspectives," 37.

13. Ibid., 38–39.

14. Nancy Veglahn, *Women Scientists* (New York: Facts on File, 1991), 123–124.

15. Ibid., 125.

TWO: BIRUTÉ GALDIKAS

1. Biruté M. F. Galdikas, *Reflections of Eden: My Years with the Orangutans of Borneo* (Boston: Little, Brown, 1995), 40.

2. Ibid., 48.

3. Sy Montgomery, *Walking with the Great Apes: Jane Goodall, Dian Fossey, Biruté Galdikas* (Boston: Houghton Mifflin, 1991), 80.

4. Galdikas, *Reflections of Eden*, 90.

5. Daniel Wood, "Persons of the Forest," *Saturday Night*, January 1988, 50.

6. Montgomery, *Walking with the Great Apes*, 170.

7. Wood, "Persons of the Forest," 50.

8. Galdikas, *Reflections of Eden*, 167.

9. Evelyn Gallardo, *Among the Orangutans: The Biruté Galdikas Story* (San Francisco: Chronicle Books, 1993), 18.

10. Galdikas, *Reflections of Eden*, 140.

11. Wood, "Persons of the Forest," 51.

12. Galdikas, *Reflections of Eden*, 319.

13. Montgomery, *Walking with the Great Apes*, 176.

14. Mark Starowicz, "Leakey's Last Angel," *New York Times Magazine*, August 16, 1992, 38.

15. Wood, "Persons of the Forest," 53.

THREE: MAE JEMISON

1. Judith Graham, ed., *1993 Current Biography Yearbook* (New York: H.W. Wilson, 1993), 277.

2. Gail Sakurai, *Mae Jemison: Space Scientist* (Chicago: Childrens Press, 1995), 13.

3. Marilyn Marshall, "Child of the '60's Set to Become First Black Woman in Space," *Ebony*, August 1989, 54.

4. "Space Is her Destination," *Ebony*, October 1987, 95.

5. Joyce Saenz Harris, "Mae Jemison: An Enterprising Woman Takes a Trek in Space," *Dallas Morning News*, February 7, 1993, 1E.

6. Maria C. Johnson, "Upward with Worldly Lessons," *Greensboro News and Record*, January 28, 1991, B-5, as quoted in Jessy Carney Smith, *Notable Black American Women* (New Haven, Conn.: Yale Research, 1992), 572.

7. Nikki Giovanni, "Shooting for the Moon," *Essence*, April 1993, 60.

8. Constance M. Green, "To Boldly Go . . . ," *Ms.*, July/August 1992, 78.

9. Harris, "Mae Jemison," 1E.

10. Ibid.

11. Veronica Webb, "No Place Like Home," *Interview*, July 1993, 75.

12. "Space Is her Destination," 94.

13. Ibid., 98.

14. Green, "To Boldly Go . . . ," 78.

15. Harris, "Mae Jemison," 1E.

16. Ibid.

17. Webb, "No Place Like Home," 76.

18. Harris, "Mae Jemison," 1E.

19. Giovanni, "Shooting for the Moon," 60.

20. Webb, "No Place Like Home," 76.

21. Harris, "Mae Jemison," 1E.

22. Green, "To Boldly Go . . . ," 78–79.

23. Jon Anderson, "Mae Jemison's on a Mission with Summer Camp," *Chicago Tribune*, April 26, 1994, Tempo Section, 1.

24. Ibid.

25. Peggy Peterman, "You Can Do It, Too," *St. Petersburg Times*, September 14, 1983, 1D.

26. Melissa Fletcher, "Beyond Beauty: Magazine Honors Former Astronaut," *Houston Chronicle*, April 26, 1993, Houston Section, 1.

FOUR: MARY-CLAIRE KING

1. David Noonan, "Genes of War," *Discover*, October 1990, 46.

2. Ibid.

3. Ibid., 47.

4. Thomas Bass, "Mary-Claire King," *Omni*, July 1993, 70.

5. Noonan, "Genes of War," 50.

6. Natalie Angier, "Quest for Genes and Lost Children," *New York Times*, April 27, 1993, C10.

7. Bass, "Mary-Claire King," 93.

8. Noonan, "Genes of War," 52.

9. Angier, "Quest for Genes," C1.

10. Noonan, "Genes of War," 48.

11. Ibid., 49.

12. Ibid.

13. Peter Gorner, "Researchers Hunting for Rogue Gene," *Chicago Tribune*, April 15, 1994, Section 1, 1.

14. "Mary-Claire King," *Glamour*, December 1983, 105.

15. Natalie Angier, "Scientists Identify a Mutant Gene Tied to Hereditary Breast Cancer," *New York Times*, September 15, 1994, A16.

16. "A Visionary Who Wouldn't Give Up," U.S. *News & World Report*, September 26, 1994, 80.

17. Natalie Angier, "The Search for a Breast Cancer Gene," *Glamour*, December 1983, 182.

18. Noonan, "Genes of War," 46.

FIVE: MARY LEAKEY

1. Mary Leakey, *Disclosing the Past: An Autobiography* (New York: Doubleday,1984), 28.

2. Virginia Morell, *Ancestral Passions: The Leakey Family and the Quest for Humankind's Beginnings* (New York: Simon and Schuster, 1995), 78.

3. Sy Montgomery, *Walking with the Great Apes: Jane Goddall, Dian Fossey, Biruté Galdikas* (Boston: Houghton Mifflin, 1991), 72.

4. Kevin McKean, "Footprints in Humanity's Past," *Modern Maturity*, February/March 1985, 78.

5. Leakey, *Disclosing the Past*, 89–90.

6. Morrel, *Ancestral Passions*, 147.

7. Leakey, *Disclosing the Past*, 96.

8. Morrel, *Ancestral Passions*, 99.

9. Ibid., 181.

10. Ibid.

11. Leakey, *Disclosing the Past*, 140.

12. Ibid., 177.

SIX: RITA LEVI-MONTALCINI

1. Marguerite Holloway, "Finding the Good in the Bad," *Scientific American*, January 1993, 36.

2. Ibid., 32.

3. Rita Levi-Montalcini, *In Praise of Imperfection: My Life and Work*, translated by Luigi Attardi (New York: Basic Books, 1988), 30.

4. Ibid., 35.

5. Holloway, "Finding the Good in the Bad," C 32.

6. Levi-Montalcini, *In Praise of Imperfection*, 85.

7. Ibid., 91.

8. Frederika Randall, "The Heart and Mind of a Genius," *Vogue*, March 1987, 536.

9. Joan Dash, *The Triumph of Discovery: Women Scientists Who Won the Nobel Prize* (Englewood Cliffs, N.J.: Julian Messner, 1990), 122.

10. Ibid., 123.

11. Ibid., 127–128.

12. Holloway, "Finding the Good in the Bad," 36.

SEVEN: SUSAN LOVE

1. "Confronting Breast Cancer: An Interview with Susan Love," *Technology Review*, May-June 1993, 46.

2. Carol Lawson, "Women as Surgeons," *New York Times*, June 29, 1987, Style Section, 1.

3. Ibid.

4. Molly O'Neill, "A Surgeon's War on Breast Cancer," *New York Times*, June 29, 1994, C12.

5. Elizabeth Gleick, "Susan Love," *People Weekly*, June 25, 1994, 147.

6. Susan Love with Karen Lindsey, *Dr. Susan Love's Breast Care Book* (Reading, Mass.: Addison-Wesley, 1995), xxvi.

7. O'Neill, "A Surgeon's War," C12.

8. Gleick, "Susan Love," 149.

9. Jane E. Brody, "Why Cancer-Free Women Have Breasts Removed," *New York Times*, May 5, 1993, Health Section, 1.

10. Love and Lindsey, *Breast Care Book*, xxviii.

11. Gleick, "Susan Love," 147.

12. Love and Lindsey, *Breast Care Book*, 75.

13. "Confronting Breast Cancer," 48.

14. Gina Kolata, "Why Do So Many Women Have Breasts Removed Needlessly?" *New York Times*, May 5, 1993, Health Section, 1.

15. O'Neill, "A Surgeon's War," C12.

16. Love and Lindsey, *Breast Care Book*, xxvi.

17. O'Neill, "A Surgeon's War," C1-12.

18. "Confronting Breast Cancer," 48.

19. Love and Lindsey, *Breast Care Book*, 24.

20. Ibid., 25.

21. O'Neill, "A Surgeon's War," C12.

22. "Confronting Breast Cancer," 53.

23. Ibid., 50.

24. Terence Monmaney, "Surgeon Who Founded U.C.L.A. Breast Center to Resign," *Los Angeles Times*, April 25, 1996, B1.

25. Ibid.

EIGHT: HELEN TAUSSIG

1. Lynn Gilbert and Gaylen Moore, *Particular Passions: Talks with Women Who Have Shaped Our Times* (New York: Clarkson N. Potter, 1981), 56.

2. Joyce Baldwin, *To Heal the Heart of a Child: Helen Taussig, M.D.* (New York: Walker Books, 1992), 20.

3. Gilbert and Moore, *Particular Passions*, 51.

4. Ibid., 25.

5. Lisa Yount, *Contemporary Women Scientists* (New York: Facts on File, 1994), 3.

6. Baldwin, *To Heal the Heart of a Child*, 26.

7. Gilbert and Moore, *Particular Passions*, 54.

8. Ibid.

9. Baldwin, *To Heal the Heart of a Child*, 57.

10. Yount, *Contemporary Women Scientists*, 6.

11. Ibid., 7.

12. Gilbert and Moore, *Particular Passions*, 56.

13. Yount, *Contemporary Women Scientists*, 7.

14. Baldwin, *To Heal the Heart of a Child*, 113.

NINE: CHIEN-SHIUNG WU

1. Lynn Gilbert and Gaylen Moore, *Particular Passions: Talks with Women Who Have Shaped Our Times* (New York: Clarkson N. Potter, 1981), 70.

2. Sharon Bertsch McGrayne, *Nobel Prize Women in Science: Their Lives, Struggles, and Momentous Discoveries* (New York: Birch Lane Press, 1993), 277.

3. Edna Yost, *Women of Modern Science* (New York: Dodd, Mead, 1962), 86.

4. Gilbert and Moore, *Particular Passions*, 67.

5. Ibid., 68.

6. McGrayne, *Nobel Prize Women*, 263.

7. Ibid., 263–264.

8. Ibid., 266.

9. Ibid., 269.

10. Yost, *Women of Modern Science*, 90.

11. Gilbert and Moore, *Particular Passions*, 69.

12. Lisa Yount, *Contemporary Women Scientists* (New York: Facts on File, 1994).

13. Gilbert and Moore, *Particular Passions*, 70.

14. Yost, *Women of Modern Science*, 80.

15. "Queen of Physics," *Newsweek*, May 20, 1963, 95.

16. Yount, *Contemporary Women Scientists*, 44.

17. *Current Biography* (New York: H. W. Wilson, 1959), 492.

TEN: ROSALYN YALOW

1. Elizabeth Stone, "A Madame Curie from the Bronx," *New York Times Magazine*, April 9, 1978, 34.

2. Diana C. Gleasner, *Breakthrough: Women in Science* (New York: Walker, 1983), 35.

3. Joan Dash, *The Triumph of Discovery: Women Scientists Who Won the Nobel Prize* (Englewood Cliffs, N.J.: Julian Messner, 1990), 41.

4. Dennis Overbye, "Rosalyn Yalow: Lady Laureate of the Bronx," *Discover*, June 1982, 42.

5. Ibid.

6. Stone, "A Madame Curie from the Bronx," 30.

7. Ibid., 31.

8. Overbye, "Rosalyn Yalow," 42.

9. Ibid., 44.

10. Ibid., 42.

11. Stone, "A Madame Curie from the Bronx," 95.

12. Dash, *The Triumph of Discovery*, 51.

13. Stone, "A Madame Curie from the Bronx," 29.

14. Ibid., 97.

15. Ibid.

16. Olga S. Opfell, *The Lady Laureates: Women Who Have Won the Nobel Prize* (New York: Scarecrow Press, 1978), 226.

FURTHER READING

Baldwin, Joyce. *To Heal the Heart of a Child: Helen Taussig, M.D.* New York: Walker Books, 1992.

Dash, Joan. *The Triumph of Discovery: Women Scientists Who Won the Nobel Prize.* Englewood Cliffs, N.J.: Julian Messner, 1990.

Galdikas, Biruté M. F. *Reflections of Eden: My Years with the Orangutans of Borneo.* Boston: Little, Brown, 1995.

Gallardo, Eveyln. *Among the Orangutans: The Biruté Galdikas Story.* San Francisco: Chronicle Books, 1993.

Gilbert, Lynn, and Gaylen Moore. *Particular Passions: Talks with Women Who Have Shaped Our Times.* New York: Clarkson N. Potter, 1981.

Gleasner, Diana C. *Breakthrough: Women in Science.* New York: Walker, 1983.

Leakey, Mary. *Disclosing the Past: An Autobiography.* New York: Doubleday, 1984.

Levi-Montalcini, Rita. *In Praise of Imperfection: My Life and Work.* Translated by Luigi Attardi. New York: Basic Books, 1988.

Love, Susan, with Karen Lindsey. *Dr. Susan Love's Breast Care Book.* Reading, Mass.: Addison-Wesley, 1990.

McGrayne, Sharon Bertsch. *Nobel Prize Women in Science: Their Lives, Struggles, and Momentous Discoveries.* New York: Birch Lane Press, 1993.

Montgomery, Sy. *Walking with the Great Apes: Jane Goodall, Dian Fossey, Biruté Galdikas.* Boston: Houghton Mifflin, 1991.

Morell, Virginia. *Ancestral Passions: The Leakey Family and the Quest for Humankind's Beginnings.* New York: Simon and Schuster, 1995.

Noble, Iris. *Contemporary Women Scientists of America.* New York: Julian Messner, 1979.

Opfell, Olga S. *The Lady Laureates: Women Who Have Won the Nobel Prize.* New York: Scarecrow Press, 1978.

Sakurai, Gail. *Mae Jemison: Space Scientist.* Chicago: Childrens Press, 1995.

Yost, Edna. *Women of Modern Science.* New York: Dodd, Mead, 1962.

Yount, Lisa. *Contemporary Women Scientists.* New York: Facts on File, 1994.

INDEX